**A Heart Of Flowers Publishing**
**Presents**

# GOING BEYOND THE VEIL

## LOOKING FOR GOD'S ANSWERS

## By Sheila T. Flowers

I pray that these words will somehow Bless you and that you will share them with someone who needs to hear that He is still in the Blessing business.

Going Beyond The Veil Looking For God's Answers
First Printing March 2003
ISBN 0-9728474-0-5
Copyright © 2002 by Inspirational Thoughts By Sheila T. Flowers

A Heart Of Flowers Publishing Co. Inc.
PO Box 670
Austell, GA 30168

Visit us at http://www.aheartofflowers.com

## Acknowledgements

Special journeys are rarely made by ourselves. I would like to thank first and foremost God who sits in heaven above. Thanks for trusting me with your Word to share with others.

On this journey you have blessed me with some earthly angels to guide me along this path called life. I would like to thank each of my nieces and my nephew for inspiring me to want to leave a legacy for you that God will bless. Thanks to my brother and sister for putting up with my preaching over the years. Thanks to each of my aunts and uncles who have stepped in to help direct my life. Thanks to all of my cousins and extended family members who have been there over the years to watch me grow into a woman. Thanks to my Godparents for listening to my TFT's every night. Thanks to all of my friends who have encouraged me to remain obedient to the call on my life (Kathy, Tomeka and Irene, love ya).

To Barbara, I say thanks for everything. You've pushed me to write a book, even when I doubted my abilities. Thanks for the many hours that you have put into making this a reality. May God richly Bless you.

And last, but not least, I would like to thank everyone who have taken the time to read my TFT's. I must thank you for your wonderful words of encouragement on a daily basis.

Always remember the only dreams that fail in life are the ones we never go after with our heart, mind, and soul.

God Bless!

*Sheila*

## Dedication

This book is dedicated to two special women that were a part of my life. Though they are no longer here with me in the physical, in the spirit we are always connected. Thanks to you mom, Janice Flowers, for giving me life. Thanks to you mama, Mattie L. Cue, for raising me to be the woman that I am and for instilling in me the courage that I have. I know that the two of you are in heaven smiling down at what I've done and I know with every rainfall there are sprinkles of your tears of joy. May God keep you in His care until we meet again!!!

# Table of Contents

# Table of Contents

# Table of Contents

# WILL YOU STILL TRUST HIM?

*I will say of the Lord, "He is my refuge and my fortress, My God, in Him I will trust."*

*Psalms 91:2*

Trust is very fragile. Unfortunately, many of us have spent our entire lives trusting the wrong people.

Some read the newspaper each day and trust all that is printed and yet they question the validity of the Bible. And furthermore, question the Omnipotence of God.

Ask yourself the following questions:

Will you still trust Him when He allows you to be put in a position that requires that you spend all that you've saved?

Will you still trust Him when your spouse turns his or her back and walks away from your marriage?

Will you still trust Him if your company hands you a pink slip today?

Will you still trust Him when the doctor says he's done all he can do and shakes his head and walks away?

Trusting God means knowing without a shadow of a doubt that the Bible is the **_unequivocal_** Word of God. Trust means that you have the faith to believe, when it would appear that all hope is gone.

Trust = Jesus

Trust = Someone who looked down through the ages and saw all that life would hand us, and made the decision to go to the cross for you and I.

Trust = Someone who walked this earth and yet never

sinned.

Trust = Someone who has held your hand and wiped away your tears when you have stayed up all night crying.

Trust = Knowing that you were His only thought on that 3rd morning when Jesus got up with all power in His hand.

So, as you get up each morning, stop and take a few minutes to tell the Lord how much you trust Him. Tell Him that no matter what may come your way, you know that as long as you have "King Jesus" you don't need anybody else.

# YOU'VE GOT TO VISUALIZE THE FINISH LINE

*I returned and saw under the sun that -- The race is not to the swift, nor the battle to the strong, nor bread to the wise, nor riches to men of understanding, nor favor to men of skill, but time and chance happen to them all.*

*Ecclesiastes 9:11*

Can you visualize the finish line? If not, get up and look a little harder. Still can't see it? Look a little harder.

Many find it hard to visualize the finish line because of the situations that we face on a daily basis. It seems hard enough to visualize the end of the day much less the actual finish line.

Could it be that God wants you to learn to not look at the present situation with your human eyes, but with your spiritual eyes, the eyes that know that through Christ **all** things are possible?

Could it be that He wants you to step out on faith? Stepping out into a place where you are secure in that if God does not give you a platform to stand on, He'll give you wings to fly?

Visualize that child on drugs turning his or her back on drugs and turning his or her life over to Christ. Visualize that adulterous husband or wife, turning from those other ways and turning his or her life over to Christ. Visualize that same abusive husband or wife taking anger management classes at your church. Visualize paying your tithes and God in turn blessing you for your faithfulness. Visualize not cursing your supervisor out for something he or she did, but instead visualize yourself receiving a praise report from that same person.

These are all things that could happen when you begin to visualize the finish line. Remember, the more you walk with

Christ, the more the enemy will attack you. He is not attacking you for the fun of it. The enemy is attacking you because he knows that if you will just endure to the end, you will get the treasures that are laid up for you in heaven.

Remember, the race is not always given to the strong, but it is given to the one who endures. So hold your head up and keep pressing on because as you visualize the finish line, you will find yourself speaking light into dark places. You will find that as your faith grows, so does God's faith in you. The more you trust Him, the more He'll give you to trust Him with. So go on and visualize the finish line, I know you can do it!

# STUMBLING BLOCKS

*Then let us no more pass judgment on one another, but rather decide never to put a stumbling block or hindrance in the way of a brother.*

*Romans 14:13*

I came today to talk about removing the stumbling blocks in our lives and replacing them with stepping stones. Taking steps toward the destination that God has for each of our lives.

I first want to talk about how we can remove the stumbling blocks by becoming stepping-stones for each other. It is not enough to say that we support each other we need to show it in our actions. There should be words of encouragement to our brothers and sisters for which God has given a vision. We need to learn to collectively support the Word of God.

For those of us with experience in certain areas we can lend advice. Not tell the person what to do, but give our testimonies for some of the stumbling blocks that we've had to hurdle in order to get to the place that God now has us. We need to help finance the vision if possible. We need to introduce each other to some of our friends who might be able to help bring the vision to pass.

Next, I want to talk about the stumbling blocks that many of us face because we choose to do things on our own. We ask God for the vision, but don't bother to ask for the details of how it is to be accomplished. The best way to begin to pick up these blocks and turn them into stepping-stones is to seek God's presence constantly. Make sure that your life is lined up with His will for your life.

Lastly, I want to talk about the stumbling blocks that many will face because they will not visualize the finish line. When God shows you the vision, ask Him to write it clear. When the vision becomes clear, then so should the finish line. God says His people perish from lack of understanding. No, you may not know or see all of the parts at one time, but trust that God is showing you what you need to know for the here and now. Take the blurred vision that is creating the stumbling blocks and use them to step forward and do what God has called you to do.

This message is very simple. There will be things in life that will cause you to fall, but the love and direction of God will pick you back up every time. Stumbling blocks that are meant to knock you down can miraculously become the same blocks that actually take you up.

So speak to that stumbling block and tell it to move and because of your belief it shall be moved. Trust God unconditionally as you step out on faith. Remember, faith is stepping out into the unknown with the belief that if God does not give you a platform to stand on, then He will give you wings to fly. So go ahead and soar to the top with God as your pilot...

# GOD IS MY REFUGE

***In God is my salvation and my glory: the rock of my strength, and my refuge, is in God.***

***Psalms 62:7***

We often hear people say that God is their refuge. Sometimes I think some people say it because they've heard others say it, but in some people you can see a light in their eyes that shows you that God has truly brought them through something. So today, I come to ask the question: Is God your refuge?

As I studied this passage, I went to Webster to get the definition of refuge was shelter or protection from danger or distress.

As I looked at this definition I could see that it was a very good definition of who God is to us. Who do you run to when danger approaches? Where do you hide when life appears to be closing in on you? Who do you turn to when the bill collectors will not stop calling your home and your job? Who do you call when it is the first of the month and the mortgage or rent is due yet the money isn't there? Who do you call?

If God is your refuge then why do many of us call on the same people every time we get in a jam? Who is your refuge God or that person? Think about this carefully. When we become so dependent on the same person to help us, then when do we call on God? Where is His place in the midst of our storm?

You see it is one thing to say that He is your Refuge, but it is another thing to know it. Knowing it means that through it all you praise Him. Praise Him in the good times and in the bad. Praise Him when you are happy and when you are sad. Praise Him for where He brought you from and praise Him for where He will take you.

Today, I did not come to give you only answers I also came to pose questions. Questions that many of us should really consider because we have become so accustomed to running to everybody for help that we miss God's solution. Sometimes struggles are His will. They don't come to destroy us, they come to make us stronger. Life will lay stumbling blocks in our paths that God will turn into stepping stones if only we will allow Him to be our refuge in all that we do.

# WHAT ABOUT ME LORD?

*Do we provoke the Lord to jealousy? Are we stronger than he?*

*1 Corinthians 10:22*

I often have times when jealousy creeps up on me. It is a jealousy that I do not even realize I have. It is a jealousy that rears its ugly head when I see others getting things that I feel I deserve. It is a jealousy that makes me quietly ask what about me Lord?

You see many of us would be quick to say that we are not jealous of anybody or anything, but is this a true statement? When no one else is around, do you secretly ask what about me Lord?

I often see God get many people out of financial jams, and I am quietly wondering if a lesson was learned. It seems that the same people seem to get into the same situations, and yet God gets them out every time. Wouldn't it be easier for Him to let them suffer just once? But it is at these times that He reminds me that He knows each of His children by the very hairs on their head, and He therefore knows their strengths as well as their weaknesses. He reminds me that what God has for me, is for me and what He has for you, is for you.

At first I thought that it was bad to ask the Lord what about me? I thought that God would be upset at my selfishness, but instead He takes and comforts me as any loving parent would when they see their child with questions. He takes me and we talk about my questions and my concerns. He lets me know that there is no need for jealousy because He is always there for me. He reminds me that too whom much is given much is required. It seems that as we look on from the outside at what appears to be a blessing, it may not always be so. He reminds me that I don't see everyone's hearts and motives the same way that He does. He

9

reminds me that He uniquely creates each person. He loves each of us so much, that where there is pain, He wants to erase it. Where there is hurt, He wants to erase it. He wants us to know that until you have truly walked the entire way in someone else's shoes, then don't ask for all that you see that they have. It might just be more than you can handle.

So today, when that little voice creeps up on you and you feel the need to ask 'what about me Lord,' think about it first. Think about the fact that you serve a God who knows everything there is to know about you. He knows all of your needs as well as your desires. Remember, the only one who should be jealous is God when our jealousy causes us to praise idol gods. So, if there is something that you think that you need, but God is not providing, then rethink the situation because the Father Always Knows Best.

# WHO HAVE YOU PRAYED FOR LATELY?

*Bless them that curse you, and pray for them which despitefully use you.*

*Luke 6:28*

It is sometimes very difficult to walk away when someone mistreats you, and it's sometimes even harder to pray for that person. But if we are going to follow Jesus' example, then pray for them we must. Therefore, I come to ask the question: Who have you prayed for lately?

Did you pray for the person who cut you off in traffic? How about the person who stole your personal belongings? What about the person who had an affair with your spouse? Or better yet, did you pray for the person who borrowed your last dollar and never paid you back?

For those of you who can quickly answer yes to the questions above I applaud you. I applaud you because it truly takes the Christ within each of us to always pray for those who cause us hurt or harm. Most of us, unfortunately, want to give hurt for hurt and pain for pain. But then we remember that Jesus didn't do that. Instead of cursing His enemies on the Cross, He went before God on their behalf to say that they knew not what they were doing. Isn't that amazing? Just imagine being pierced in the side, a crown of thorns, being beat all night long, yet He prays for them anyway. What an awesome God we serve!!

Learning to pray for your enemies, instead of cursing them, demands that the flesh must die. Why? Because we all know that the flesh wants to fight every fight, but the spirit within knows that every battle is not yours to fight. Learn to pray for them instead. Allow God to right any wrongs that need it. Don't be God's little helper because He can handle it all by Himself.

So today, when someone mistreats you, go to God in

11

prayer. Your prayer shouldn't be for revenge, it should be for God to step in and do what's right. Remember, the Word says "*But love your enemies, do good, and lend, hoping for nothing in return; and your reward will be great, and you will be sons of the Most High. For He is kind to the unthankful and evil. Therefore be merciful, just as your Father is also merciful.*"

So, again, I ask the question: Who have you prayed for lately?

# FINGERPRINTS FROM THE HEART

**Bind them upon thy fingers, write them upon the table of thine heart.**

**Proverbs 7:3**

In today's world there is a certain image of what a person should or should not look like to be termed "beautiful." We have more beautifying techniques on the market than I could probably count. We can change everything about ourselves except our fingerprints.

Fingerprints are the one feature that God will never allow us to change. It is that one constant reminder that says you are uniquely designed. You are His designer's original. Your fingerprints are from His heart. He gave you those particular fingerprints to remind you of the love that He has especially for you. Because they are unique they can never be mixed up, just as His love for you can never be mixed up.

Some of us find it very difficult to understand how God could love us when we've done so many things wrong. He is a God who loved you before you ever knew Him. He loved you so much that He made sure that He gave you something that would always remind Him that it was you. It doesn't matter how low you've fallen in life, He still knows that it is you. He is a God who will pick you up because your fingerprints are His designers' signature. He is a God who is willing to come get you exactly where you are, not where you pretend to be, but exactly where you are. He gave you your particular fingerprints from His heart as your means of identifying the love that He has for you.

Some of us have walked with God a long time. There have been times when we have fallen, but because of our fingerprints He was able to quickly say that one is my child, so let me help them up. He has proven time and time again that all that He has is ours. He has been there when we've been hurt and He was able to pick us up. He has

13

taken our fingerprints and held them up to the mirror when we question our looks, our life's goals, or our situations. He has shown us that He has made us exactly the way that He wants us to be through our uniqueness.

Take a few minutes to really think about your individual uniqueness. There may be some features that you are not happy with and God does allow changes. But remember that sometimes it is not the physical appearance that needs to be changed when looking in the mirror sometimes it is the spiritual appearance that requires the change. There are some changes that only the Master Surgeon can perform, but throughout it all He will never allow one change. That one change is your fingerprints. Your fingerprints should always be that one reminder to you, that there is someone in this world who loves you more than anybody else. He loves you unconditionally. He has always been there for you, even before you were ever thought of. So every time you begin to question things about yourself, look at your fingerprints and know that you have a God that loves you so much that He designed you to be an original.

## CAN YOU REACH MY FRIEND?

*And when he comes home, he calls together his friends and his neighbors, saying to them, 'Rejoice with me, for I have found my sheep which was lost.'*

*Luke 15:6*

How many people have some particular person or persons that they have been praying would turn their lives over to the Lord? You've stood in the gap praying without ceasing. Today we come collectively to ask the Lord can you reach my friend?

There are many people who have known the Lord at some point in their life, but due to various reasons have slid back into the world. There are some who have never known the Lord, but your lifestyle keeps them curious about the goodness of God so they hang around in hopes of meeting Him. Some spend their entire lives running in the opposite direction of where they think the Lord is residing. But today, we come boldly before the throne with our request that the Lord reach out His hand of mercy in hopes that our friends might accept it.

Some of us have fasted, prayed without ceasing and laid prostrate before the Lord, but it seems that a breakthrough isn't going to happen. Hold on, because His delay is not a denial. That same person who you are praying for, is just like the prodigal son who at some point came to his senses and realized all that his father could offer. This is the same thing that will happen to our friends and loved ones as we continue to stay on bended knees. Just when it would seem that change is impossible, never lose sight of the God who can make anything possible. Know that your praying is not in vain. Know that your breakthrough is on the way.

So today, be encouraged that the Lord does hear your fervent prayers. Know that the shortest distance to any solution is the distance from your knees to the floor. No problem is out of the bounds of God's mighty reach, so know that He can reach down and pick your friends and loved ones up out of their searching. Know that He is the solution that they are searching for, and He is there waiting with arms outstretched. So get prepared *and when he comes home, he calls together his friends and his neighbors, saying to them, 'Rejoice with me, for I have found my sheep which was lost.'*

# SAVE THE LAST DANCE

*And David danced before the LORD with all his might; and David was girded with a linen ephod.*

*2 Samuel 6:14*

How many of us have heard the saying saving the best for last? Did you ever consider the Lord within the same thought? Do you know that when you've done all that you can do the Lord will save the last dance for you?

The Lord saves the last dance for us a great deal of the time. There are times that we waltz around the dance floor with Him because we do not want to totally release our issues to Him. There are times when we dance back and forth with Him by giving it to Him to work out then going back and grabbing it before He is finished. There are times when we slow dance with Him because we continue to take baby steps in our Christian walk when He is trying to get us out of the lamb stage and into the sheep stage. There are times when we become so tired of dancing that He picks us up and twirls us around the dance floor. He always saves the last dance for those of us willing to step onto the dance floor with Him.

Stepping out onto the dance floor with the Lord is the best dance you will ever have if you trust Him totally. Just as in any dance, there has to be a person who is allowed to lead and you therefore must choose who will be the leader in your dance? As you allow Him to lead you around the dance floor, you have to take your cue from Him on which direction to go. The directions can be found in His Word. You have to be in tune with your dance partner to know when He is going to turn you around. Being in tune comes from having a personal relationship with Him. It comes from knowing that if He turns you around then there is obviously something better in the other direction. Next, in your dance, you have to know when to stop. The Lord has sent the Holy Spirit to dwell within us, to show us when it

17

becomes time to stop those things that are blocking our blessings. The Lord is willing to dance with you all night long if necessary, and when it appears that you are getting tired, do remember that He will carry you off of the dance floor.

So today, if you've danced with the Lord, but you decided to lead instead of allowing Him to lead, then go and dance with Him again. This time, in your dance, allow Him to lead and see if the outcome becomes different. You see He is Alpha and Omega. The Beginning and the End. He gave you your first dance lesson as He pushed you out of the womb. He continues to dance with you in every storm in your life, but you've just got to learn to let Him lead. Saving the best for last ensures that, one day, you will get to have the last dance in person as He says well done my good and faithful servant.

# IF YOU ONLY KNEW

*They said to him therefore, "Where is your Father?" Jesus answered, "You know neither me nor my Father; if you knew me, you would know my Father also."*

*John 8:19*

Sometimes as I listen to people talk about the happenings in their life I wonder if they realize how good God has been to them. Many give God continuous praise, but many complain the entire time. I often listen with the thought going through my mind "if you only knew."

In life, we tend to praise God for those things that we see Him doing in our lives, but what about the things we never see? Do you ever take time to thank Him for dangers seen and unseen? What about the life you lived before He saved you in which you knew death should have gotten you first? What about the hand that He extends to your family who falls under your prayer of protection? If you only knew those things which He saves you from day in and day out?

If you knew all that God does for you, would it cause you to praise Him more? If you knew how much He truly loved you, would you cherish the relationship more? If you knew that tomorrow was not promised to anyone, would you accept Him today?

Sometimes, in life, we have to step back and look at the big picture. We need to step back and realize how God orchestrates our blessings. We need to step back and realize that Jesus sits at the right hand of the Father day in and day out, interceding on our behalf. Though we've given our life to Christ, many of us still backslide, day in and day out, yet He continues to bestow His grace. If you only knew...

Today is the day to stop taking God for granted. Stop looking at His blessings as your rights, but begin to look at them as the privileges you've been given by Him. God is a good God. He is a God that knows you like no one else. So next time you are about to complain, think again about His goodness and you will begin to understand why I said, "if you only knew."

# IF YOU WERE NEVER BROKEN

*The sacrifice acceptable to God is a broken spirit; a broken and contrite heart, O God, thou wilt not despise.*

*Psalms 51:17*

Were you broken the day that you turned to Jesus? Do you have things in your life now that sometimes appear to break you? If so, do you know that it is all a part of His master plan? You see, if you were never broken, then how do you know that He can make you whole?

Many of us had so many problems in our lives that we realized only Jesus could help. We found ourselves living lifestyles that were not pleasing. We found ourselves unable to manage our finances. We found ourselves worshiping idol gods. We found ourselves broken.

For some, it was something they heard someone say at church that caused them to come to Christ. For some, it was something they heard on a television ministry. For some, it was how they saw you living your life. For some, He found curled up in a corner calling on His name. For some, God is knocking at your heart will you let Him in?

You see it doesn't really matter how you found Christ, the important thing is that you did. As you gave your life to Him, He has slowly, but surely, began to mend the broken pieces. He has taken you, the broken vessel, and is doing a work in you daily. All He requires is that you give Him all of you, not just the parts that you want changed, but all of you. Know that He will make you anew, if only you would trust Him.

So today, if there are parts of you that are broken, then ask Him to heal you. Ask Him to make you whole. You see, in order to truly worship Him, then He needs the whole you. He needs you to be whole so that He can introduce you to a lifestyle that is pleasing to Him. He wants to show you how to handle your finances His way. He wants to show you that He is the only One you should worship. It is through your brokenness that He will show you why He is the Potter and you are the clay. So, stand back and watch Him put all of the broken pieces back together again and you will find yourself a new designers' original.

# FOREVER RUNNING

*...running stubbornly against him with a thick-bossed shield;*

**Job 15:26**

I've met some people over the years that have spent a lifetime looking for the answer, which has always been before them. They have spent a lifetime running from here to there, yet never able to grasp the answer. Do you know that until you accept Jesus into your heart as your Lord and Savior, you will be forever running?

For those of us who have accepted Jesus as our Lord and Savior we realize that it was because of His grace that we were allowed to stop running. It was His grace that kept us as we searched in every place, but the right place. Many of us searched in the clubs, many of us searched in fornicating relationships, many of us searched in our bank accounts, many of us searched in the liquor bottle. Many of us searched everywhere before we decided to search our heart. You see Jesus has always been in our heart; we just never looked there for Him.

For those of you who have never accepted Jesus as your Lord and Savior my heart bleeds for you because I realize that you will be forever running. You will always be running trying to find Him. Many will not stop when He calls. Many will hear yet never hearken unto His voice. Many will stop and give it a little try, but then slide back into their old world. If you understand nothing else in life, understand that you are still here because of His grace. It is His grace that keeps you as you try everything that you are big and bad enough to try. You know those things that you do, that only the two of you know about. Know that His grace sustained you, yet you still turn your back. How many chances will you have since tomorrow is not promised? Think about it!

So today, know that there is someone who can make sure that you are not forever running. If you accept Him into your life, know that He will keep you in good times and bad. He will keep you as you keep Him in your heart. Therefore, if you want to stop running and rest, then know that you can find rest in the arms of Jesus if you accept Him today.

# AND IT WAS GOOD

*And God made the beast of the earth after his kind, and cattle after their kind, and every thing that creepeth upon the earth after his kind: and God saw that it was good.*

*Genesis 1:25*

Do you ever look in the mirror and wonder why does God love me so much? You see all of your shortcomings, but He still whispers that He loves you. Do you know that when He looks at you, He smiles and says it was good?

God looked down through the ages, even before the foundation of the earth and knew that one day you would be born. You would be born to look the way you look and be exactly who you are. He knew that you would have frailties. He knew that you would have shortcomings. He knew that some of us would be born into families who did not know Him, and yet we would. He knew that some of us would become drug addicts, some drug dealers, and some prostitutes. He knew that some of us would take jobs only for the paycheck and not really tap in to our God-given talents. He knew some of us would accept Him, yet never walk with Him. He knew all of this and yet He looks at you and continues to say and it was good.

Remember, no matter what you are going through or have gone through, Jesus' blood on Calvary guaranteed that you would be able to rise above any circumstance in life. He knew that His blood would be more addictive than any drug. He knew that He could offer you much more than selling drugs ever could. He knew that one day you would stop prostituting yourself because you realized that your body was a holy temple. He knew...

All that you are was allowed so that you could one day turn your life over to Him. He does not make our decisions for us. He allows us to make our own decisions: some good, some bad, but all our choice. It does not matter what decisions you have made before because now is the time to make the only decision that truly matters and that is to give your life to Christ. He will forgive your past. He will mend all of the broken pieces. All it takes is that one step of faith.

As you look in the mirror today ask God to show you the beauty that He sees. It is not a physical beauty that makes Him utter and it was good, it is a spiritual beauty. If we could begin to see ourselves as He sees us, then we could truly begin to walk into our destiny. Know that everything that God has created is good and you are His designer's original. So whenever you begin to doubt yourself, remember that when God looks at you He's saying and it was good...

## AFTER THE TEARS ARE GONE

*May those who sow in tears reap with shouts of joy!*

**Psalms 126:5**

Crying sometimes seems to be the most logical thing for us to do when situations are beyond our control. When storms are raging to and fro, many of us truly go into our corners for a good cry. What do you do after the tears are gone?

I don't think that there is anything wrong with crying, just don't do it too long. You see I feel that God does sometimes allow us our pity parties, but at some point we have to stop the crying and move on with our lives. How do you handle these situations? Did the crying solve the problem? Did you somewhere in the midst of your crying realize that your God is bigger than your problems?

After the tears are gone, the same God who was there to wipe away your tears is still there to help you get up. Some of us forget that God does not leave us we leave Him when things don't go our way. He is faithful to us, even when we are not faithful to Him. When storms are raging we forget that He is our shelter. Just as He cared enough to wipe away the tears, He is also there to show us our life lesson if only we would look. He is there to show you that after the tears, joy does come.

How many of you truly realize how precious your tears are to God? They are so precious to Him that He stands with His arms open, waiting for you to run into them and turn all of your problems over to Him. The abusive spouse. The failed relationship. The unkind word that was said. The unhappy job. The out-of-control kids. The doctors report. All of these things are ones that He is waiting for us to give to Him, but instead of turning them over to Him many of us try to handle them ourselves. Yes, God does give us the ability to handle situations, but He has also said that He will always be there for you. Wouldn't it be better to turn everything over to Him, rather than waiting until everything is out of control?

So today, I say to you after the tears are gone, hold your head up because joy does come in the morning. It does not matter what your problem may be because our God can fix it. It may not be the way you would have fixed it, but His way is better anyway. So you have two roads you can take to resolve your problems, one road is the short road, which is to turn everything over to God, or the long road, which is to try to do it yourself? You decide which one you will travel.

# BEING USED BY GOD

***It shall not be poured upon the bodies of ordinary men, and you shall make no other like it in composition; it is holy, and it shall be holy to you.***

***Exodus 30:32***

One of my favorite things about the Old Testament is the way that it shows ordinary people being used by God. I like this because many of us are under the impression that we have to be perfect before God will use us. This is not true and the Old Testament gives proof.

Take a look at Moses. Moses was just an ordinary person that God used in a mighty way to lead his people out of Egypt. Look at King David, the shepherd boy, who was coined as a man after God's own heart. King David proved that when you fall down, you could repent and get back up and get in line again. How about Job, who was coined as God's faithful servant? Even though Job lost everything, he stated that he would still trust God. None of these people were great before God called them. These were just ordinary people, who believed in an extraordinary God. Their belief in God earned them a spot in the greatest book ever written, which is the Bible.

Do you think that God can take ordinary you and use you in a mighty way? What is your definition of being used mightily and are you willing to go the extra mile for your Big God? You see God needs servants who are faithful to the call on their lives. He needs someone who is not afraid to go into the at-risk areas and lead someone to salvation. He needs someone who is not afraid to go into the inner-city schools and make a difference. He needs someone who is not afraid to stand up and be a real Christian. Is this you?

So today, know that being ordinary to man, does not mean that God sees you just as an ordinary person. He looks through His spiritual eyes and sees all of your potential. He sees that recovering addict as a mighty prayer warrior one day. He sees the ex-prostitutes walking the streets selling Jesus instead of selling their bodies. He sees and He knows that if you ever begin to truly trust Him then you will see that the job that He has assigned you is not just an ordinary job, it is your special job assigned to you by Him personally. So step up and answer the call that He has on your life and allow yourself to be used by God.

# NEVER GIVE UP

*Create in me a clean heart, O God, and put a new and right spirit within me.*

*Psalms 51:10*

One of the topics that God has been laying on my heart for a while to address has been suicide. I've tried to skirt the issue because I have never been able to fully understand what would make someone consider ending their own life. It is through the grace of God that I now speak to the people who have considered suicide as an option. Remember, to never give up on Jesus because He will never give up on you.

As God began to minister to me on this subject I had to try to pay close attention. God began to speak into my spirit some of the things that would cause someone to want to end their lives. Things such as the loss of a child, an abusive spouse, a failed marriage, unloving parents, feelings of not being loved, deep bouts with depression or feelings of struggling with homosexuality. All these things plus many more cause people to consider giving up. May I offer Jesus as your way out?

You see Jesus loves you just as you are. He is willing to mend all of the broken pieces because He is the Potter and you have to allow yourself to be the clay. Those things that happened in the past can be healed. Nothing has happened in your life that Jesus can't see you through. No problem is so minute that He will ignore it. He is always waiting with His arms outstretched for you to come. He is that one, true person who you can tell all of your deep, dark secrets and rest assured that it will go no further. He is so loving, so much so until He will come exactly where you are. Not where you pretend to be before the world, but exactly where you are. He designed you to be an original. He knows you by name. He knows the very hairs on your head. Who could know so much about you and still not care? He is offering you His never-ending love, if you would only accept it.

So today, I say don't give in to Satan. Don't allow Satan to convince you that Jesus doesn't care because Jesus does. If He didn't, I would have no need to write this thought. If only one person receives this thought and it causes them to change their mind about suicide then this message was for you. You see God will send a thought to thousands of people just to get one person's attention, just to show you how much He cares. So never give up on Jesus because He will never give up on you!

## JUST GOING THROUGH THE MOTIONS

*For the LORD your God has blessed you in all the work of your hands; he knows you're going through this great wilderness; these forty years the LORD your God has been with you; you have lacked nothing.*

*Deuteronomy 2:7*

Do you ever sit back and wonder if life has more to offer than you are currently experiencing? Are you sometimes on the outside looking in at the person that you've become? Are you just going through the motions?

There are some of us who have lived our entire lives and have yet to find happiness. We exist, but we don't actually live. We let life pass us by because we are focusing so much on our wants, that we overlook what we have. We forget that happiness is a choice that we have. We forget that we decide if we will see the glass half full or half empty.

Some of us are so busy going through the motions, that it has become commonplace. Those things we once dreamed about are dreams of the past. We think that where we are is where we are meant to be. We think that God wants us to settle for less. This is not correct. God wants the best for you. He knew that some of you couldn't handle college when you were younger, but now you are able to simply because you are older and more determined. He knows that some of you are very restless because you want to be self-employed. If God says so then go with your dreams. He knows that some of you are tired of being mother and father to your children, therefore ask Him for your joy back because children are a blessing from Him. Ask Him to help you attain your dreams and to help get your life in focus.

Going through the motions is not always good when you are at a restless point in your life. You can see the dream, but yet you can't quite touch it. God has promised, but you doubt that it will come to pass since it has been so long. Just keep praying and holding your promises in your heart. God is an On-Time God. Trust that He knows exactly what you need, when you need it. Just make sure that you are preparing yourself for the blessing!

This thought is to encourage you to live life to the fullest. Dreams that God has given you, that He has said will come to pass, will do exactly that. If He has promised you, then it is so. God wants all of us to see our true potential. Just because you are short on funds today, doesn't mean that you will be that way tomorrow. He needs to make sure that you can handle the small finances before He can give you the larger amount.

Just because many of us are in the wilderness wondering when it is going to be our turn to see the Salvation of the Lord, know that you already have because even in the wilderness the Lord your God is there taking care of you and you shall lack for nothing.

## FAILING THE TEST

*But we pray God that you may not do wrong--not that we may appear to have met the test, but that you may do what is right, though we may seem to have failed.*

**2 Corinthians 13:7**

Does life sometimes feel like just as you weather one storm another one blows in? It sometimes feels like the storms are never-ending. Do you realize that we continue to see the same test because we continue to fail the same test?

As you take and begin to look at the storms in your life, do you see a pattern? Do you see a recurring storm? Normally, in life when you see the same storm continuously, it is usually a sign that you keep failing. Sometimes we fail the test put before us because we are looking to learn one lesson and God is trying to teach us a different lesson. Sometimes we fail because each time the test is put before us we use our natural vision and not our Holy Vision. Sometimes we fail because we refuse to bring our flesh under control. Sometimes we fail...

Finances seem to be a big issue with the children of God. We find ourselves constantly struggling. What test in your finances is God putting before you that you are continuing to fail? What are you doing wrong in your finances? Is it that He allows the struggle so that you learn how to manage a little before He can give you a lot? Is it that He wants you to learn the difference between a want and a need? Is it that He wants you to trust that He will see you through?

Looking with our Holy Vision usually denotes putting our complete trust in God. It shows our sign of faith. It shows that we believe that if we step out into the unknown with our trust in God, then He will either give us a platform to stand on or wings to fly.

Bringing our flesh under control can be very difficult, but not impossible. Bringing our flesh under control requires our faithfulness in putting aside things that block our blessings. It requires not putting ourselves in a position where our actions are misunderstood. It requires not re-creating old relationships that are harmful to our current relationships. It requires putting one foot forward, so that God can move you two steps ahead.

Failing a test in life can be difficult because we usually see it over and over again. No matter what test is put before you, God does expect a certain answer and until we get the correct answer we continue to see it. Whatever you are doing in life that continues to take you in a never-ending circle, cast it out today. Ask God to show you the testimony that goes with the test that you continue to fail. You see, if you never get the test answered correctly, then you never get to move on to the next level. Going higher in the Kingdom of God is what it is about, so ask the Master what is needed to pass the test.

# HE HEARD MY CRY

*Hearken to the sound of my cry, my King and my God, for to thee do I pray.*

*Psalms 5:2*

Crying is an outlet that we all use to let out the emotions that we have bottled up inside of us. Sometimes they are tears of joy and sometimes tears of pain. Do you recall the first time that you called on the Father and He heard your cry?

I think back to being in high school and it was the last day of my eleventh grade year. I was very excited about taking the SAT the next morning and about finally being a high school senior. Little did I know that my world would come crashing down that night as my grandmother explained to me that my mother had just died. A world that seemed so full of hope all of a sudden became a world of despair. I remember just sitting and crying. I wasn't exactly sure how to pray the right way, but a calmness came over me as I poured out my heart to God. I prayed that somehow my mother had made it into heaven. I prayed that somehow the Lord would help me get through. It was then that I first learned that He truly heard my cry. It was then that I realized that even though I didn't understand why, I trusted that He knew best.

I think back to my last day at Florida A&M University. I was very excited about graduating the next day, but I was also very nervous about what tomorrow held. I had spent the last 5 years growing up in Tallahassee, FL. The friends and professors I met at FAMU had both schooled me and educated me. I reflected upon the person I had become. I reflected upon the fact that God had heard my cry. He had sent me an extended family to take care of me as I healed. He had shown me that joy does come in the morning because I was preparing to walk across the stage and receive my MBA. What an awesome God. Instead of tears of pain at this graduation, I now had tears of joy.

Many of us think that God does not hear us when we cry. He does. Though there are times in life when He will allow the struggles and storms in our life, know that there is a bigger picture. Know that there is victory in sight. Just when you think that you've done all you can do, pray some more because He does hear your cry.

So today, if they are tears of joy or tears of pain, they are both to make you stronger. They are tears that God is willing to personally come and wipe away, if only we would ask. So don't think that what you are going through does not matter to God because it does. Allow Him to be the light unto your feet to lead you out of your storm because no storm is so fierce that He cannot step forward and say "Peace Be Still" and they not obey. So remember to call on God to say *Hearken to the sound of my cry, my King and my God, for to thee do I pray.*

# AFTER THE STORM CLEARS

*He made the storm be still, and the waves of the sea were hushed.*

*Psalms 107:29*

Do you ever feel bad about the doubt that you had during a storm in your life? A part of you believed that God would see you through and the other part held on questioningly. What do you do after the storm clears?

There is one thing about God and that is His assurance that storms don't last always. Oh, storms come and they go, but they are only temporary situations. The problem that occurs is that some of us act up so badly during the storm and then we are forced to feel guilty after the storm clears. We want what we want exactly when we want it. We believed that God would handle everybody else's problem and not ours. We show Him our true colors. We call on everybody for prayer, when God has already promised.

Because storms come and they go, we should all get to a point where we learn in whom to put our trust. We should begin to realize that God can and does have our blessings waiting for us on the other side of our storms. You see if you learn to weather the small storms by trusting Him completely, then the foundation is already laid for the bigger storms.

After the storm clears we are reassured that God had it under control all of the time. Some storms last longer than intended because of the way that we handled it. Some storms end quicker because we weathered it with our complete trust in Him. You see the storms that come are building blocks. The building blocks are replacing the old blocks so that we become a new building because our body is the temple of God. We need to make sure that our foundation is steady.

So today, after the storm clears in your life, look back on it and make sure that you learned a lesson. Take your understanding of your lesson to God in prayer, so that He can validate your findings. You see it would be a shame to miss the intended lesson because we all know that if you fail a test then you will see it again. So remember, that there does come a time when you get to an "after the storm clears" in your life and you have the reassurance that you can look back and say *He made the storm be still, and the waves of the sea were hushed.*

## ACCEPTING RESPONSIBILITY FOR WHO WE ARE

*If you do well, will you not be accepted? And if you do not do well, sin is crouching at the door; its desire is for you, but you must master it."*

*Genesis 4:7*

Are you happy with who you are? Do you think that there are some things in your life that need to be changed? Do you blame other people and circumstances for who you are? Now the time has come for each of us to accept responsibility for who we are.

It is sometimes very difficult to accept responsibility for who we are because though we live in the present we blame the past. We blame our parents. We blame the school system. We blame our neighborhood. We blame our church. We blame history. We blame everybody except for the person in the mirror.

Many of us choose not to blame ourselves because to do so means we have to accept some of the responsibility for who we are. Life seems to be a little more acceptable in our sights when we can blame others. How long will you live this way? How long will you allow the past to dictate the future? If God woke you up this morning, then live today going forward. If you have a criminal record, but you are now reformed, then pray and ask God to send you to an employer who will give you a chance. Don't blame others if you fall a few times. The key to getting to the finish line is getting back up.

Many of us can't stop blaming others because we choose to live with the pain rather than letting it go. We choose to stay mad with our parents for not being good parents instead of talking honestly with them about the hurt. They may not be able to offer you the healing that you desire, but trust God that the first part of your healing process is being able to communicate the pain to the ones who inflicted it. Even if you weren't the smartest child in school but you have a desire to learn, then enroll in an adult education course. You have the ability to achieve all that your mind can conceive, but it requires taking a step forward. If you don't attend a church because the last one hurt you somehow, then pray and ask God to send you to one that will fulfill your needs. There is more than one church out there and God has work for you to do.

So today, as we begin to put the past behind us, it first comes with accepting responsibility for who we are. Though others might have contributed to the pain in the past, you determine your future. As you allow God's will to lead your life you will find that putting the pain of the past behind becomes a little easier because as you walk with God, He allows more of His love to heal your past. So don't continue to blame others. Move forward knowing that your future is secure with Christ as the head of your life.

# DON'T STAY IN THE STORM TOO LONG

*He made the storm be still, and the waves of the sea were hushed.*

*Psalms 107:29*

Storms will blow in and out of each of our lives. Some storms are for a moment, and yet some last longer. The problem occurs when many of us choose to stay in the storm too long.

I know many would not agree that they choose to stay in storms, but many times we do. We choose to stay in storms when we refuse to forgive our parents for not being good parents to us when we were young. We refuse to forgive the first person that broke our hearts. We refuse to find a new church because the last one hurt us. Don't stay in the storm too long.

The devil will do things in our lives that many of us choose to carry around for the rest of our lives. Because many of us were not born with silver spoons in our mouths, like some friends, we blame our parents. We blame our parents because instead of being home to raise us, they were in the streets. We blame them for not being home when someone molested us. We blame them...

Know that God has seen all that you have gone through and He is still allowing you to stand today. All of the things that your parents unfortunately did not give to you, He is waiting to show you how, as a parent, you should handle those situations. I'm not saying that your parents did not do the best that they could do, quite the contrary, but know that God has always been there. Learn to lean on Him. Ask Him to show you how to forgive the past and move on with your life. Don't stay in the storm too long.

Don't spend the rest of your life being angry at the first person that broke your heart. I know it is even more difficult

43

if you have a child from that person because everyday is a reminder. Know that what the devil sought to destroy you with, God has turned around for your good. Take that child and bless God everyday for their existence. It might not have been in your plans for your life, but know that it was in God's Holy plan. So keep your head up and know that God will continue to see you through. Remember, that weeping may endure for a night, but know that joy does come in the morning. Guess what? It's morning time!

I've met a lot of people over the years that have made the statement that they are just not doing church right now, and most of the time I choose to be silent and just listen. You have got to listen and understand what has caused the pain before you can begin to minister to the problem. You see, many of us want to remind the person to not forsake the assembling of the saints, which is true, it says so in the Word, but hear the person out first. Let's step back from our judgment and try to see it through that person's eyes. It might just be that in listening you might be able to show the person how every church is not the same. Many, many churches truly are out to edify the body of Christ. Many churches are out to heal the wounded. We've got to be able to direct them to a place where they can feel the presence of God. We've got to first make sure that they have a relationship with Him. As their relationship grows, trust God to help them get back up and get back in line. So, if this is you then don't stay in the storm too long.

Today, I pray that you do not stay in your storm too long. There is a lot of pain in many of our pasts, but know that God is a healer of the past, present and future. Talk to Him about your storm and ask Him to get you out. Trust that if He allowed you to go into a storm, then surely He is the One to get you out of the storm. Just ask and expect that He will tell the storms to be still and the winds will hush, so that you can move on with your life. Remember, as you turn your storms over to Him, it is when we see His greatest works in our life. Because surely if you give it to Him, then He'll handle it!

44

# CAN I CHANGE MY YESTERDAY?

*Jesus Christ is the same yesterday and today and forever.*

**Hebrews 13:8**

How do you mend yesterday's hurt with today's love? Can I change my yesterday?

The only option to healing yesterday is to trust Jesus Christ who is the same yesterday and today and forever. Jesus is the only other person that knows all of the pain that your yesterdays inflicted. He is the only one with the authority to make the storms cease in your life. In order for Him to take full control you've got to hand it over.

You see many of us walk around with so much hurt and pain created by our past. Though we've moved on in life, the hurts have only been buried and not healed. We've offered God our hurts of today because we don't want to live through Him healing our pains of yesterday. Just as any physician will tell you, in order for any bruise to heal you've got to take the bandage off. The bandage that covers the bruise will never allow it to heal completely, just as the pains of yesterday are hidden in their private little corners that we refuse to take the bandage off. How can God heal you if you don't show Him where you hurt?

Facing your yesterdays changes the outlooks for today about your yesterday. You see God will heal your yesterday. He will take what you once saw as you being victimized in some way and turn it into your victory. He will heal the hurt from an unloving parent by showing you His unconditional love. In life when man "will not or cannot" love you the way that you want, trust that God will know how to love you unconditionally. Through His love and healing process your yesterdays become your testimonies for your tomorrows.

45

So today, if you want to change your yesterday, then allow God to take the bandage off. Allow Him to change those old, hurtful memories into loving testimonies. Allow Him to show you how to forgive your past in order for you to embrace the love that your future holds. So look up, because God can change your yesterdays because *Jesus Christ is the same yesterday and today and forever.*

## JESUS WILL PICK YOU UP

*Humble yourselves before the Lord and he will exalt you*

*James 4:10*

Some people think that the Lord only accepts those who are "good" people. Many think that their past eliminates them from any type of acceptance into the Kingdom of God. Do you realize that Jesus will pick you up?

I must say that man is very judgmental. Many of us think that you have to be of a certain caliber before we can interact with you. You must be in a certain family before you sit in a certain area in church. You must have a certain income level to be considered wealthy. You must belong to a certain club or organization to be accepted. Whose judgment matters the world or God's?

You see God does not care who your family is. He does not care where you sit in church, just get up and go to one that fills you spiritually. He does not care about your income limit because His streets are paved with gold. He does not care about your skin color. He does not care which club or organization you belong to. All He cares about is that you come to Him with an open heart and He is willing to pick you up just as you are.

Because God is not a respecter of persons, He is able to see past your past and pave your future. He is willing to come and pick you up out of your circumstances and send you in the right direction. Remember, He does allow U-turns. He will take what looks to be a bleak future and turn it into a God-purposed future. A God-purposed future is the one that He has planned for you. It is the one that takes circumstances from the past and uses them as stepping stones for the future. Jesus will pick you up.

So today, if it appears that you don't have what it takes to become a child of God, then think again. You see, God is willing to accept you as you are. Black, white, red, or yellow, God doesn't care. God knows that it takes many colors to make a beautiful rainbow. So today, if you think that you are not good enough, then look in the mirror and know that Jesus says come as you are. You take the first step and trust me, He will lead the rest of the way.

# SEARCHING FOR ANSWERS

*But from there you will seek the LORD your God, and you will find him, if you search after him with all your heart and with all your soul.*

*Deuteronomy 4:29*

As we go through life, we often try many other things before we try the Lord. Many of us live day-in and day-out always searching for something in hopes that one day we would get a clear message. We are always searching for answers...

Though God has always been there for us, many of us, probably most of us, took the long route to finding out exactly who God was. Many of us searched in the clubs, many of us tried different denominations of churches, many of us made our spouse or mate our god, we searched in the alcohol bottle, we searched in the drugs, we searched all over for answers. Then one glorious day the Lord spoke to our hearts and some of us answered, while others are still searching.

This was the first step to answer God when He called you and the next step is to search for answers. The answer to all of life's questions can be found in the Word of God. You find that as you give of yourself in the understanding and learning of the Word, the more the Lord trusts you with. The problem that occurs is that we want the answers, but we don't want to do the research. We want God to speak and therefore we would never have to seek. Unfortunately, this is not the case. The bible states, *But seek ye first the kingdom of God, and his righteousness; and all these things shall be added unto you.*

As you study the Word and you begin to gain an understanding of the Word, next you should begin to focus on your personal relationship. Make sure you get to a point where you know His voice. One of the worst things in life to

49

have is God giving you answers, yet you don't know His voice and therefore do not hear Him. So work on developing your own relationship.

So today, as you search for answers, know that there is one place where you can find all of your answers which is the Bible. God's Word does not come back void. So as you begin to open your heart to God, know that He will bring your searching to an end. Therefore, remember and don't forget, *But from there you will seek the LORD your God, and you will find him, if you search after him with all your heart and with all your soul.*

# THE POWER OF THE TONGUE

*Keep your tongue from evil, and your lips from speaking deceit.*

*Psalms 34:13*

Did you know that it takes just as much time to tear someone down with your tongue as it does to build them up?

Unfortunately, many of us are quick to speak and slow to listen. We fail to realize how the small things that are said are sometimes the big things that tear us down.

We forget that we should teach our sons how to love as they become men and not just go from childhood to manhood without ever learning how to love. Unfortunately, many young men are raised to believe that a man does not cry, but even Jesus wept. Teach your son all of the aspects of being a man.

Teach your children through positive use of your tongue. Teach them through continued positive reinforcement. Encourage them to be all that life has to offer. Challenge them to be different. Challenge your children to go the road less traveled. Teach them when you discipline them. It's OK to discipline them, just make sure that they know why they are being disciplined. Make sure that they understand that you still love them. All this can be accomplished with positive affirmations of your love to them. Allow yourself to show your children unconditional love, even when they are wrong. Raise them to be God-fearing children. Sometimes all it will take with your children is just for them to hear you say that you love them. Try it because you never know how that child's life might be turned around.

Unfortunately, many of us have ruined a few relationships because we refused to hold our tongue. We just had to say what was on our mind, instead of asking God how to handle the situation. Had we taken the route of praying first, God might possibly have turned the entire situation around in both of your favor? Remember, He is an awesome God.

Remember, David the Psalmist said, *"Let the words of my mouth and the meditation of my heart be acceptable in thy sight, O LORD, my rock and my redeemer."* This is how we should be. The words that should come from our lips should be positive. We are children of the most High God. The world is supposed to be able to look at us and see the Christ in us. Can they see the Christ in you? If so, what picture of Christ are you painting?

When we wake up each morning, we should be asking God how to speak something positive into someone's life? The world needs to know that Jesus spoke things into existence. He did this with the power of the tongue. He raised the dead, He made the lame walk, the blind see, and He healed bodies from infirmities, all through the speaking and the laying on of hands. So, as you go about your day and you find yourself in a situation where you are about to say something negative, stop and think... What Would Jesus Do?

# LET'S SET THE ATMOSPHERE

*Behold, I send an angel before you, to guard you on the way and to bring you to the place which I have prepared.*

*Exodus 23:20*

Did you know that as a child of God, when you are at work, you should be able to set the atmosphere?

In our daily walks with God, many of us leave Him at the door when we get to work. I know many would disagree with this statement, but I think there is a lot of truth with this statement. Ponder the thought for a minute.

When co-workers are complaining, instead of telling them how blessed they are that they have jobs many of us join the complaining. We forget the fact that unemployment rates are ridiculously high. We forget that we prayed and asked God for the job that we are now complaining about.

We need to step back and take a few minutes to communicate with God. Ask Him why He sent us to this particular place? You are not at this job by accident. God sent you there to affect someone else's life, but unfortunately, we are spending so much time complaining that we missed the test that was put before us.

Remember, God can give you any job, any salary, any company, so why did He choose the one in which you have? There has to be an ultimate reason.

Is it to learn to deal with all types of personalities, in order for you to handle what He has in your future?
Is it that particular salary so that you can manage a little, before He gives you a lot?
Is it to show upper management in Corporate America that you will stand up for God anywhere?

53

Your presence at your job should dictate that of respect. The anointing on your life should be one such that you continue to set a positive atmosphere. Don't get caught up in the office politics. Don't get caught up in the clique's at work. Don't get caught up in the office gossip.

Get caught up in showing the world exactly who Jesus is. Show the world how you live and present yourself when Christ is the head of your life. Remember, you are the head and not the tail. You should be able to lead and not always follow.

So as you go to your job each day, go knowing that you are on a special assignment from God. Go forward knowing that if God has sent you, there is a bigger purpose. Get up each day asking Him to show you which atmosphere needs to be changed, and go forth setting the atmosphere.

# WHO WILL BE REMOVED?

*He changes times and seasons; He removes kings and sets up kings; He gives wisdom to the wise and knowledge to those who have understanding;*

*Daniel 2:21*

Have you noticed that God allows some people to enter your life for only a season? Some of us find it difficult to understand when a certain person is no longer in our lives. Maybe they didn't leave by accident? Maybe God removed that person from your life because they had deposited all that they were supposed to deposit.

Holding on to relationships is not always a good thing. When God's grace has been removed from the relationship, He leaves us with the option to stay or leave?

Unfortunately, many of us stay and then ask God why certain things are happening. I am not saying that a particular person did not enter your life for a specific reason because that I am sure of. The problem occurs when we start taking more from the relationship than God intended.

Some men and women enter our lives to show us what love is, some to show us what love isn't, but, ultimately, they were never intended to stay. Some of us have supervisors who show us what good management is, what good management is not, but, ultimately, we need to learn to work with anyone. God will allow many people to enter our lives in order for us to learn a certain lesson in preparation for some future test. Letting go is not always easy, but being in a relationship without God's grace is far worse.

God removes certain people or things from our lives when they become our gods. There are certain relationships where we begin to stay home with him or her on Sundays rather than going to the house of the Lord, even though some of us found him or her in the church. There are certain good-paying jobs that God allows to give us pink slips in order for us to understand where the blessing actually comes from. So take a step back and ask God who or what needs to be removed from your life. Ask God what is hindering your blessings?

So, as people enter and exit your life, take some time to ask God for their purpose in your life. Remember, for everything there is a purpose. Learn where you can learn and teach where you can teach, but ultimately remember too whom much is given, much is required. How much are you willing to give God in order for Him to move you to your next level? Be prepared, because it just might require the removal of someone very close.

# HOW DO I WALK AWAY?

*Order my steps in thy word: and let not any iniquity have dominion over me.*

*Psalms 119:133*

How many people find that it is hard to walk away from the past? Relationships, jobs, friends, family, church, etc.

There are times in life when walking away is the only option. That unequally yoked relationship where you are moving in one direction and they are moving in another. You want one thing out of life and they want another. How do you turn and walk away?

What about the job that stopped challenging you years ago? Do you stay there because you are almost to retirement, or do you walk away and do something that brings your joy back? How do you walk away?

What about those friendships that seem to keep going up and down? One day you are friends and the next day you are not. Do you stay in that friendship when it causes more hurt than happiness? Is this one of those who will be removed? How do you walk away?

What about the family member that continues to borrow all that you have? Do you continue to lend them the money, car, time or do you step back and allow God to be God? How do you walk away from what you've done for so long?

What about the church that you stopped growing spiritually in many years ago? Do you stay there because that's the only church that you know, or do you move on to a new church where you will have spiritual growth? How do you walk away?

Walking away is not easy, staying is sometimes worse.

When a situation no longer has God's grace, is it better to stay or leave? There are times when God is saying, walk away, and there are times when He is saying stay, but unless you have a personal relationship with Him you have no idea what He is saying.

God will allow us to stay in things as long as we would like. It is up to us to listen when He says go. We should not get mad when things continue to go in the wrong direction, when God has given us His direction.

I didn't come today to say walk away, I came to ask the question "how do you walk away?" I too have asked this question many times and always heard the Lord say "*But seek ye first the kingdom of God, and his righteousness; and all these things shall be added unto you.*"

That's the key. Seek God for the answer. There are times when He will have a delay in His response. There are times when you will miss God's answer. There are times when you will stay regardless of His answer to you, but know that God is God and He will always answer the prayers of the righteous. He answers in His time, not ours. Just wait for Him.

So how do you walk away? Ask God to order your steps and the walk becomes that much easier.

# GOD ALLOWS U-TURNS

*For if you return to the LORD, your brethren and your children will find compassion with their captors, and return to this land. For the LORD your God is gracious and merciful, and will not turn away his face from you, if you return to him.*

**2 Chronicles 30:9**

I've often laughed when I've heard the saying that you can't teach an old dog new tricks. I've come today to propose that you can teach an old dog new tricks simply because God allows U-turns.

New tricks can be taught to anyone. It can be taught to the person who has been in church all of their life. It can be taught to the person who has been in the world all of their life.

God gives grace daily. With each day come His brand new mercies, mercies that can change your life for the good.

The first thing that we have to recognize is that *through Christ **all** things are possible*. Seasoned Saints need to remember that God will use anybody who is willing to be an open vessel. It is possible for God to send a young person to your church and you actually learn from that person and vice versa.

Sometimes it is best to sit back and observe before we take offense to what someone is showing us. Remember, God gives each of us talents and gifts. He also will send us help, even when we do not think that we need it.

A person who is still in the world does not think that someone who is no longer of the world can tell them what to do. They forget that we haven't always been saved. They forget that God allowed us to make U-turns in our life.

Think about a U-turn. It means that you were headed in one direction and then turned completely around. This is what happens when you allow Christ to lead your life. It means that things that you once did not have a conscience about, you now have.

Most of the time when we make a U-turn when driving it is because we are headed in the wrong direction or we missed our turn. Look at life in the same manner. If you know that you are headed in the wrong direction, make a U-turn. Just remember, God is waiting at the finish line to say, *"well done my good and faithful servant."* Therefore ask yourself if you need to make a U-turn in order to make it to the finish line because God does allow U-turns.

# WHEN WILL HE ANSWER?

*Only two things do not do to me, Then I will not hide myself from You; Withdraw Your hand far from me, and let not the dread of You make me afraid. Then call, and I will answer; Or let me speak, then You respond to me.*

**Job 13:20-22**

One of the hardest things for many of us to do in life is to wait. When we are going through the waiting process many of us find ourselves questioning God. We are saying to Him that we've been good and faithful, so where is His end of the deal? We sometimes forget that it is truly a process.

The following 10 steps can help you to endure while waiting on God:

1. Be content to know that God is always in charge
2. Acknowledge that God is with you
3. Keep fellowship with believers
4. Know that God sets and knows your limit
5. Wait for God's perfect timing and not your own
6. Trust in the Lord to guide in the right direction
7. Wait upon the Lord
8. Seek the truth always
9. Keep pure and a clean heart
10. Always look to the Lord for your help

When the storms are raging in your life and you are waiting on God for an answer, BE PATIENT. Know that God is in control. His delay is not a denial. God is faithful and He is just. If He has said that it is so, then count on it. Remember, God is not a man that He should lie.

So the answer to the question "when will He answer?" is simply this: in His own time and His own way. Allow God to be God. He does not need your assistance in giving you an answer. He does not need your advice. Just step back and let God be your guide and I guarantee you will get an answer.

## ARE YOU WAITING ON GOD?

*I am weary with my crying; My throat is dry; My eyes fail while I wait for my God.*

*Psalms 69:3*

Has God promised you something that has yet to come to pass? Do you still believe that if God said it, then it is for you? Are you waiting on God?

Many of us hold promises in our heart that God has told us, yet they have not come to pass. The question becomes, are you taking the steps to get where God is sending you? God is the master architect of your life. He stood before creation and designed you to be a certain way. He knew the bumps that you would go over in life. He knew the winds that would blow in your life. He knew that you would make promises to Him that you wouldn't keep, but because He is God He cannot and does not tell a lie. Therefore, if God said it then it is so.

As you wait on God are you listening for all of His directions? If He promised you the house, have you spent the last year cleaning up your credit report? Have you spent the last six months paying all of your bills on time? Have you prepared yourself for your blessing? You see, sometimes in the waiting process, God is telling us to make preparation because everything that He does is good. How can He bless you with the house now, when He knows you cannot handle that responsibility, and therefore you must wait?

What about your call to the ministry and the recognition that you want? Have you started with the basics by being an example? Remember, ministry is not just about being in a pulpit, it is about spreading the Gospel everywhere you go. God needs to know that you can go to the places that no one else is willing to go. He needs to know that you will

63

be an open and willing vessel. So, until you are where He wants you to be, you must wait.

I want to make sure that this message is very clear. Many of us are waiting on God for an answer, and we sometimes get discouraged because it appears to be taking too long. Please know and understand that God is preparing you while in the waiting process. He is making sure that you have the disciplines in place to handle the blessing that you are about to receive. So listen to His instructions very clearly. He will walk you through the steps to get to the blessing that is waiting for you.

So today, if it appears that you are waiting on God, ask Him what you need to do in the meantime. God's promises are always fulfilled. There is sometimes a delay, but if He promised you, then there is never a denial. All He needs is for you to follow His directions and you can't help but end up in the right place. So trust that His Word is one that you can truly stand on.

# WHY ARE YOU CRYING?

*Now why do you cry aloud? Is there no king in your midst? Has your counselor perished? For pangs have seized you like a woman in labor.*

*Micah 4:9*

There have been times when I have cried due to the pain in my life. The pain from the death of a love one, severing of different relationships, unhappiness on the job, and just making life-changing decisions. They are sometimes tears of joy, but mostly tears of pain. As I look back on the situations I have to ask myself, why were you crying?

You see some of us are so accustomed to crying when there is pain, we forget that some pain actually brings joy. We look at the death of a loved one as pain and yet we sometimes forget how that person suffered here on earth due to an illness. We sometimes cry when our spouse or mate walks away from our relationship, when in reality there are times when we should actually be dancing. Many of us cry out to the Lord because of our unhappiness on the job, yet we forget that this job is not about us, it is about the lives that God wants us to affect. Life-changing decisions can sometimes be painful. Stepping out into the unknown comes with it's own set of fears, if we allow it. As we make life-changing decisions, we must remember to bring God into the equation in the beginning, to make sure it balances itself out.

I am not negating that sometimes these pains bring tears, but know that God resides in the midst of your pain. It is when we are weak, that He is strong. He understands better than anyone what you are going through, but know that joy does come in the morning. God is there to be your counselor during these times. He is there to tell you how to get back up and get back in line. You see life does present obstacles that seem insurmountable, but if God is your track coach, you can hurdle any obstacle. You just have to trust that He will bring you through.

So today, as you sit with tears in your eyes because of some storm that is creating pain in your life, know that God is there. He is there to show you that as you get through this storm, there's a rainbow on the other side with a blessing with your name on it. So, cry if you must, but in all that you do remember to praise God because He has promised to never leave you, nor forsake you. And if He has said it, then it is so!

# I WAS THAT BROKEN VESSEL

**Has the potter no right over the clay, to make out of the same lump one vessel for beauty and another for menial use?**

**Romans 9:21**

Do you know that there was something about most of us that was broken which brought us to Jesus? Do you know that He is the Potter? Do you know that He can take you as a broken vessel today and turn you into beautiful pottery?

As you walk with God, you should grow with God. Some of us become so mature in God, that we forget that we were once broken. This can be good and this can be bad. It's good because God will make you anew each day, but bad because sometimes we leave our testimonies behind.

Do you know that when someone who is struggling looks at you, they can't see how they can ever measure up? They see themselves and feel that God can't change them. They do not realize that you and I were once broken vessels.

As I've often listened to testimonies, I've often wondered where in the testimony did God get His glory. Because surely if He brought you through your test, then He should get the glory. Because so many of us appear to have it "going on", broken vessels become intimidated. They don't realize that God is a God who will come where you are. He will come to the "crack house," He will come to a broken home, He will come to the job, He will come into the hospital, He will come...

When we lie before the Lord in our broken state and call on His name, we are acknowledging that He is bigger than our problems. We are acknowledging that we know that no problem is too small that He does not care. It is our brokenness that allows God to bring forth our beauty.

You've got to be broken before you can be used. God has to train you. He has to be able to trust you.

Some of us like to do it the hard way. We like to run from the call on our lives. We like to be like Jonah and go to Tarshish instead of Nineveh by way of the belly of the fish. If God has called you to do anything, then step forward and do it with boldness. If He has called you, then surely He has equipped you. Draw courage from the brokenness that has been mended by the Potter.

So today, thank God for the brokenness. It was through your brokenness that you allowed God to step in. He came to you exactly where you were. For those of you who have not surrendered your life to Christ, then do so today. He will accept you as a broken vessel, but when it is all over you will come forth as pure gold.

# GOD IS BIGGER THAN YOUR PROBLEMS

*And God is able to provide you with every blessing in abundance, so that you may always have enough of everything and may provide in abundance for every good work.*

### 2 Corinthians 9:8

There are times in life when we must admit that some things are better left to someone with more experience. We must accept that our problems are big. We accept this because we know that we serve a God who knows all and that God is bigger than our problems.

As I spend time thinking about the Omnipotence of God, I realize the limitations of my mindset. I look and I see what appears to be mountains, but my God looks and sees anthills. My problems, that sometimes overwhelm me, should truly be turned over to the Lord.

I think back to all the blessings and storms that I have had in my life and I truly know that I still stand because God knew me long before I ever knew Him. God knew me when I watched my grandmother die of cancer. God knew me when I decided to move to Atlanta and start over. God knew me when my job decided that they would relocate to Florida. He knew that I would worry about not having a job, yet He still loved me. He knew that I would try to handle everything on my own, yet He still loved me.

Just as God knows me, He also knows you. He knows that you may not have the money for the car payment this month, but if you trust in Him then He'll make a way. He knows that the kids need clothes for school. Trust in Him. He knows that your job is planning a layoff. Just trust in Him. Trust that God is bigger than your problems. Trust in Him in all that you do. You can't serve Him only when things are going wrong, acknowledge Him in all your ways. Trust that

God is...

**Jehovah-rah:** *your caring shepherd*
**Jehovah-jireh:** *the Lord who provides*
**Jehovah-shalom:** *the Lord of peace*
**Jehovah-rophe:** *the Lord who heals*
**Jehovah-nissi:** *the Lord my banner*

Trust that God is the great Jehovah. No problem when turned over to Him comes back without a solution. Develop a relationship with Him such that you understand no mountain is high enough nor any valley low enough that He will not come to your rescue because He is bigger than your problems.

So today, I charge you to take it all to God. Lean on Him. Trust in His word. Trust that the bigger your problem, the bigger your God. He will do exceedingly and above all that we may ask, but it requires your trust in Him. Will you trust Him?

# THE SCREAM THAT WILL NOT BE HEARD

*There is no speech, nor are there words; their voice is not heard;*

*Psalms 19:3*

Some of us walk around so frustrated. We continue to hold everything inside of us. We feel that we can best deal with our own problems, in our own way and do not need help. Do you know that you have a scream that will not be heard?

I know we all want to handle our own issues. We feel that given enough time and given certain conditions then we can work them out on our own. We keep everything so tightly wound until God has difficulty trying to unravel us. We are unhappy in our marriages. We are unhappy in our jobs. We are unhappy with our children. We want to go somewhere and just scream, but instead we hold it inside.

Holding everything inside is not always wise. There are many of us that go to church every Sunday and dance all over the church, then still leave unhappy. We can pray for someone else and watch it come to pass. We can handle everyone else's problems, yet our own go unanswered.

We hold it inside until it begins to eat away at us. The unhappy marriage that should have been turned over to God has now become the marriage that you've finally just walked away from. The unhappy job that we should have turned over to God to find out our purpose for being there, we walk away and just quit and abort our true purpose that God had intended. Those children that we made sure got everything they wanted and are now spoiled and rotten and we can no longer control them, we should have turned them over to God long ago to ask Him how we should have raised them. These things that we have allowed to eat at us because we didn't want to turn them over to God, are now destroying us on the inside.

Turn them over to the one who can help before they get to this point. If they are already at this point still turn them over. No problem is irresolvable when you enter God into the equation. If Jesus could go into the grave for three days and resurrect with all power, then know that your problem is resolvable. If Jesus could stay in the wilderness for 40 days and still not be tempted, then know that your problem is resolvable. Don't continue to allow your problems to eat away at you and bring about illnesses. Jesus has said that He will always be there. So trust that He is always there for you and let that scream come out as you pour it all on the altar to Him.

# LETTING GO OF WORLDLY THINGS

*For the weapons of our warfare are not worldly but have divine power to destroy strongholds.*

*2 Corinthians 10:4*

When I first turned my life over to Christ, I thought that I could change everything over night. I thought that all of those fleshly desires would come under submission that same day. Then reality set in, I realized that some things would be a struggle, but all could be done. I realized that if I wanted to let go of worldly things then it would require a change on my part.

Many of us have been saved for a long time and still have not brought many of our fleshly desires under submission. I will be the first to admit that this is not always easy, but I will contradict in the same sentence and say they can be done when we ask God to help. Many of us continue to do some of the same old things and blame it on the devil. Did he make you do it, or did you really do it yourself? Be honest and lay blame where it truly should be.

As we grow in Christ, we should leave many things behind. We should leave behind the heavy drinking, the use of drugs, adultery, fornication, pornography, profanity, gossip, back-stabbing, lying, cheating, stealing, debt, bouncing checks, etc. We should leave behind anything that does not bring a smile to God's face. I know some habits are hard to let go, and with the list above I know we were all pinched somewhere. God wants His children to act as if they are His children. What example are you showing the world when you can out-curse someone in the world. Or even worse, you, the child of God, starting the office gossips. How about you, the Pastor, sleeping with a member of your congregation? Or you, the Saint, stealing from God when you don't pay your tithes because you saw an outfit you wanted to buy instead? Let's stop allowing the worldly things to control who we are. Let's realize that we are children of the Most High King and begin to subdue some of these worldly desires. No, we are not perfect, but each day our walk with God should be leading us closer to Him and not closer to the devil.

Today's thought is not to throw daggers at you it is to remind you that we all have some things that we need to let go. The day that we accepted God into our hearts, He sent the Holy Spirit to dwell within us and we therefore should have a conscience of our wrongdoing. Understand that God is a forgiving God, but is it true repentance when you keep doing the same thing? It is as if you ask for forgiveness, but your fingers are crossed behind your back. Ask God to help remove your fleshly desires, which are those things that threaten your chance to walk upright. When you show God that you truly want to change, not just say it, but actually mean it, then count on Him to show up and remove those desires. You see He knows each of our weaknesses and He wants to help, but we need to ask for it. Because just as surely as you ask, then He will help!

## HE'S ABLE

*Now unto him that is able to do exceeding abundantly above all that we ask or think, according to the power that worketh in us, Unto him be glory in the church by Christ Jesus throughout all ages, world without end. Amen.*

### Ephesians 3:20-21

Many of us spend a great deal of time worrying about things for which we have no control. We worry from sun-up to sun-down, sometimes with a little crying in the middle. We spend so much of our time worrying, we forget that for everything we need in life, He's able.

God is able to supply all of your needs. God sees so many of His children worry over finances. We worry if we will have enough money for groceries. We worry if we will have enough to pay the mortgage or rent. We worry if we can make the car payment. We worry if we can pay the insurance. We worry so much that we lose focus of our Faith Maker. We forget that God is...

One of the things that I have observed with my Christian brothers and sisters is that we take it to God, but then we still worry. We take it to God, but then we get on the phone and call around for assistance. We take it to God and promise this is the last time that we are going to misuse our money. We take it to God, but we come up with our own alternatives. So the question becomes are you truly trusting God to provide your need or are you calling on your family member or friends that you have made into your god? Taking it to God means trusting it to God. Trusting that He will see you through. If you are going to worry, don't pray. If you are going to pray, then don't worry. God is...

One of the other things that I have observed and probably experienced firsthand in some situations is that we conclude that God did not provide when the package does not come in the wrappings that we wanted. We

75

wanted Him to give us all of the rent or mortgage money, but He only gave us a portion so that we would understand the testimony that came with the struggle. You see God does always answer His children, but just like any parent it is not always the answer that we want. There are times that He is able to do more than He does, but He will reply to you that His grace is sufficient. Is it sufficient enough for you?

Know and understand that God is able to supply over and above all that we may ask. It first begins with trusting Him. Trusting Him to know what is good for you and what is not. It next begins with learning from the trial that you have gone through. If you find yourself continually coming up short in your finances, then know that somewhere along the line you keep failing the test. Ask God to show you how to make your finances meet your needs. It might hurt a little, or maybe a lot, as you make adjustments to your lifestyle, but the end result is far better than the recurring struggles. So ask Him to help. Ask God to make you wise in your finances because it does little good to give you millions of dollars when you can't manage the hundreds that you have. So ask for wisdom in your finances and watch how that one blessing leads to many more. So don't forget that *now unto him that is able to do exceeding abundantly above all that we ask or think, according to the power that worketh in us, Unto him be glory in the church by Christ Jesus throughout all ages, world without end.*

# QUIET TALKS WITH GOD

*The words of the wise heard in quiet are better than the shouting of a ruler among fools.*

*Ecclesiastes 9:17*

How many of you have very long days? You get up in the morning running and it looks like that is the pattern for the entire day. When do you find time for your quiet talks with God?

I've come to realize that each night as I sit at my computer, it has been reserved as my quiet time to have my talks with God. It either begins with Him directing me to which scripture I need to read or sometimes it is just me talking about my day. I sometimes find myself very tired as I write because I'm usually gone for at least half of the number of hours in the day. Because I'm in management I've usually dealt with some type of problem or problems that sends you off on some type of tangent. But once I get home and I am able to sit, then the Lord caresses me. He helps me to relax. As I begin to relax it is then that He speaks to me about the next inspirational thought. Do you find the time to let Him caress you into relaxation?

Quiet talks with God are my chance to speak from my heart. It is my chance to lay prostrate before the Lord and worship Him. I am able to thank Him for all that He has done. I am able to thank Him for His mercy. I am able to thank Him for His grace that sustains me.

I often wonder how I ever functioned in life before I met the Lord. Having to live a life of searching for that someone who is right in front of you. Searching for that place of peace. Searching for a God who will come to you if you ask Him to. Have you found Him? Does He meet you in your quiet place? Do you have your quiet talks with God?

Finding a place where you have quiet talks with God is

important in your daily walk. It is in this place that you learn to hear His voice. It is in this place that you have a two-way conversation. It is in this place that His silence means He's listening and that you have His undivided attention. If you don't have this place, then I invite you to find one. If you offer God the invitation, He will show up.

So today the choice is yours. You can start your day running and never take the time to have your quiet talks with God or you can realize the importance of your time spent in His presence and make the appropriate changes. Remember, *The words of the wise heard in quiet are better than the shouting of a ruler among fools.*

## YOUR GIFT TO GOD

*For by grace you have been saved through faith; and this is not your own doing, it is the gift of God -- not because of works, lest any man should boast.*

*Ephesians 2:8-9*

A friend gave me a picture that says that life is our gift from God, what we do with our life is our gift back to God. What is your gift to God?

Unfortunately, many of us walk around as if God owes us something. We sometimes forget all that He gave us on the Cross at Calvary's Mountain. Therefore, if we were to truly look within, we should be asking ourselves should we expect more than the chance of salvation then we have already been given? Which is salvation that we can't earn because it is free to all who accept Jesus as their Lord and Savior. It is God's gift to us, now the question becomes, what is our gift to Him?

Many of us have been blessed with beautiful singing voices, yet we never sing praises to God and wonder why we've never been discovered. Some of us write so eloquently and have such a way with words, yet we never write anything that gives God glory and then wonder why none of the publishers will respond. Some of us have a talent with children, yet we never volunteer our time to help the youth and then wonder why we don't feel fulfilled. Some of us are very talented artistically and we do some arts that reverence God, yet we keep the other foot in the world, and then wonder why our talents never see their full potential. We give all that we have, just to the wrong person...

What we have to realize is that God gives all of us talents. He gives us talents that should be used for His glory. There is something that your hands combined with your heart can do, that will bring a smile to God's face. Once we truly sit back and think about where all gifts come from we should gladly give God His portion. Take your talent and uplift His kingdom. You might not get the glory on earth, but remember that there are treasures stored up for you in heaven, and God does reward the faithful.

So today, I ask that each of us look within ourselves and ask what gifts are we giving God? God gave us our talents for a specific reason. Don't be selfish. Use them to glorify Him. The more you are about handling God's business; the more He will be about handling yours. So stop giving the world all of your talents and give them to God. Ask Him to guide you in the uses of your talents, so that your use lines up with His will. If you allow God to guide you, then you can never go wrong. So go ahead and make God smile.

# A FRIEND WHO STICKS CLOSER THAN A BROTHER

*A man who has friends must himself be friendly, but there is a friend who sticks closer than a brother.*

**Proverbs 18:24**

Everybody in life needs somebody else. Though some have tried, none have successfully been an island. Human interaction is a healthy outlet in life. The key to successfully managing in this world is to remember that though many will enter and exit your life there is only One who sticks closer than a brother.

Though many of us have family and friends that we love dearly, somebody within these categories has hurt us at some point in our life. Some of the hurt was intentional, but some of it wasn't. Through the hurt came broken relationships, some repairable and some irreparable (or so we think). Some of us have been quick to forgive, while others of us have held on to our un-forgiveness. Just thinking about the old wound causes new pain. Can I offer a Friend who sticks closer than a brother? He is a Friend that will never let you down. He is a Friend that is able to heal your past, present and your future, if only you would allow. He is a Friend and His name is Jesus.

In our lives many of us are caught off guard when someone walks away that we care for dearly. Some of us are devastated when we lose a loved one. Some of us are distraught when relationships become broken. Have you ever given thought to the fact that everyone that enters your life was never meant to stay? Some people were only meant to teach a specific lesson or to teach several lessons, but that person's intent in your life was never long-term. I know that this is hard for many of us to understand because losing someone, no matter what the situation, can be difficult. Though it is difficult, you have one Friend who has promised to never leave you. So as many enter and exit, put your trust in the One who will never leave.

As you go through this journey called life, lean on the spirit within to help you understand a person's entrance and exit in your life. If we begin to focus on what that person offered us, instead of what we expected, then we can begin to put the experience into focus. Everybody that enters your life is there for a reason: good or bad. From this lesson, learn and grow and grow and learn.

So today, as you spend quiet time in the presence of the Lord, thank Him for those who entered and exited your life. Pray and ask for understanding of why they were there in the first place. The key to not having tests repeated in life is to learn from them the first time. So though you allow many into your life, always keep One Special Friend present in all of your relationships and that is Jesus. Keep Him there and lean on Him because *a man who has friends must himself be friendly, but there is a friend who sticks closer than a brother.*

## SOMEBODY PRAYED FOR YOU

*But I have prayed for you that your faith may not fail; and when you have turned again, strengthen your brethren.*

*Luke 22:32*

There are many people who are reading these thoughts who do not know how to pray for themselves. Many of them have been blessed beyond measure, yet how could this be when they never take the time to pray? Many are surviving because somebody has prayed for them.

There are many of us who are living off of borrowed prayers. Some of us are living off of the daily prayers of others. And some of us are operating in the red.

Borrowed prayers are those prayers that grandma, grandpa, mama, daddy, etc. said for us over the years. The prayer warriors are long gone and many of us are still being blessed because of their prayer life. There are many of us who received our foundation in the church at young ages and now we have allowed the worldly foundation to complete who we are. The God that we worshiped as a child is now a debatable issue to many. Understand that He is the same God that your grandma prayed to. He is the same God who keeps you daily from dangers, seen and unseen. He is the same God that protects you and your family. He is the same God that held your hand as you cried, when you buried your grandma. He has allowed you to survive so that you could make a rational decision and turn your life over to Him before grandma's prayers run out. The choice is yours...

There are many of us who have relationships with others who keep us held up before God in prayer. It might be a spouse, boyfriend or girlfriend, sibling, friend, co-worker, etc. You see whether many of us realize it or not, there is someone praying for us. They are praying that we will accept Christ as our Lord & Savior before it is too late. They are praying us through each of the storms that rise up in our life. They are there. The question becomes will they always be there praying for us, if not, how will we survive the next storm?

There are many who are operating in the red (in the negative). You don't pray for yourself and your friends have walked away. God has spoken to the heart of those praying for you and said that now it is your turn. God is calling you to come into His presence. It's OK if you don't know how to pray just trust God to show you how. All it takes is for you to bend your knees and He'll help you do the rest. You can get through it. Heaven never closes and God never sleeps nor slumbers. So take the time to start your own prayer life today.

Prayer life is important. It is through your prayer life that you speak to the Father through His Son Jesus. It is where you begin to develop a personal relationship with the Father. There is no need to be scared because remember if He kept you and loved you in your sin, then surely He will love you as you turn your life over to Him. For those of you who are prayer warriors, then stay on bended knees because God does reward your faithfulness. So today, remember when you see yourself being blessed and yet you know that you are not praying, know that it is because somebody has prayed for you.

# IN THE TWINKLING OF AN EYE

*...in a moment, in the twinkling of an eye, at the last trumpet. For the trumpet will sound, and the dead will be raised imperishable, and we shall be changed.*

*1 Corinthians 15:52*

Life can sometimes be seen in the twinkling of an eye. If you do not believe me, ask the person who walked away from a car accident, where the car was totaled, yet they had no scars. Ask the person who walked away from a burning home that is fully engulfed, and yet there are no burns. Or better yet ask the person whose medical diagnosis was initially a negative report, and yet the doctors cannot explain why all of a sudden the symptoms no longer appear.

It is when we feel that we have heard the last trumpet in our lives that we truly can see how awesome God is. We can see how in the twinkling of an eye our lives flash before us. We can see then how God has spared us for a purpose.

Many of us sometimes take life for granted. We think that we will live long enough to make all the decisions at a later date. We think that if we stop going to the clubs and start going to church we will lose our friends. We think about everything except where we will truly spend eternity. We think that today is not the day that we shall be called home. We think...

Unfortunately, God does not present us with the timeline that shows when our journeys on earth will end, so many wait until it is too late. At this point the decision of where you will spend eternity has already been made.

Please know and understand that God has a plan for each of our lives. He has called each of us to serve Him in some manner. We are to serve Him in spirit and in truth. We are to serve Him with gladness in our heart.

In the twinkling of an eye your life can be flashed before you. The question becomes is your soul lined up with the Will of God? Is the flash a sign to change some things in your life? Look back on your life and ask God why He spared you? Talk to Him about His purpose for your life. You see He could have chosen anyone to be called home, and yet you He spared. Why? Take some quality time and get to know Him. It is a relationship that you will never want to lose once you truly have it!

# IT CAUSES ME TO TREMBLE

***...tremble before him, all the earth; yea, the world stands firm, never to be moved.***

***1 Chronicles 16:30***

Sometimes, I just sit and think about all that the Lord has done for me. I think about the blood He shed on Calvary's mountain. I think about how He has always kept me from dangers seen and unseen. I think about all of the inhabitants of the world and how many turn their back on Him. I think about all that He continues to do for us in spite of what we do and it causes me to tremble.

I tremble because I ask myself the question: Am I truly worthy? I wish that I could honestly yes that I am worthy, but reality is that I am not. There have been times that He has told me to do something, and I knew without a shadow of a doubt it was God and yet I still did not do it. There have been times when He has said go left, but I went right anyway. There have been times when He has said give more of yourself, but I found an excuse not to. I could spend the next year or more, if I were honest with myself, admitting all that I've done wrong. Yet He still continues to love me. If I were to take my wrongdoings, along with all of yours, and we each add them together, then we should truly ask why Lord do you still continue to love us? We should each begin to tremble.

You see, we serve a God who is willing to look past our faults. He is a God who still continues to use us. He is a God who is always willing to come and get us when we call on the name of Jesus. His goodness is so great that it causes me to tremble. You see He knows our faults before we ever commit them, and yet His love is everlasting. What a mighty God we serve.

Today, think about all of the things that God has truly done for you and you too should begin to tremble. You see those things that He has done; He didn't have to do them. He could have allowed us to endure the life that we so richly deserve, but He did not. So give thanks and remember who is Lord. Never forget to *tremble before him, all the earth; yea, the world stands firm, never to be moved.*

# GOD ORCHESTRATES YOUR BLESSINGS

*And God is able to provide you with every blessing in abundance, so that you may always have enough of everything and may provide in abundance for every good work.*

*2 Corinthians 9:8*

Some of us in life are so blessed that we sometimes mistake it for what it truly is. We have become so accustomed to God's unmerited favor that we fail to properly take time to thank God for all that He does for us. We fail to remember that God orchestrates our blessings.

Many of us go to the doctor at least once a year and never give thought when we receive a clean bill of health. We fail to thank God because everybody's doctor report is not always good. Many of us go to work and get our paychecks, pay all of our bills and never give thought to those whose paycheck did not quite cover everything, much less the many that do not have jobs. Many of us come home to our house or apartment and turn on the air or heat and never give thought to the people who sleep on the streets. Many of us...

You see, many of us have become so accustomed to our current lifestyles that we sometimes fail to realize that these are all blessing orchestrated by God. Sometimes the simple things that we have in life, which are commonplace to us, are dreams for others.

God demonstrates His love for each of us daily. It does not matter what all is going on in our life, regardless of all our situations, He does demonstrate to us daily. Each day the sun does rise, each spring the flowers do bloom, each year we do get a rainy season to replenish nature. Each day babies are born to replenish the lives that are no longer here. Just as one person is crying tears of joy, there is someone somewhere else crying tears of pain.

So today, I say look at God's blessings for what they are. He wakes you up every morning and you in turn should take time to thank Him. He allows you one more chance to right some wrongs. He allows you to go through situations that make you stronger. He gives tests often in which <u>you</u> determine if you pass or fail. Each day His judgment seat of mercy declares His grace has already covered you. So stand strong each day knowing that He does orchestrate your blessings.

## SILENCING JEZEBEL'S VOICE

*Then Jezebel sent a messenger to Eli'jah, saying, "So may the gods do to me, and more also, if I do not make your life as the life of one of them by this time tomorrow."*

*1 Kings 19:2*

When most people think of Jezebel, the wife of King Ahab, the first thing that usually comes to mind is her make-up. It was believed in the old days that Jezebel's make-up was what made her evil, they did not realize back then that it was not the make-up, but a spirit. A spirit so evil that through her voice she was able to send a prophet of the Lord named Eli'jah to hide in a cave. I've come today to silence Jezebel's voice.

Jezebel's voice is the one that always brings doubt. It is that voice that is constantly reminding you that your blessings will not last. Well today, going forward, we choose to silence her voice. We boldly step forward renouncing all that she has to say.

Many people have fallen prey to Jezebel's voice because they do not recognize that spirit for what it is. When you get a promotion that you know you didn't deserve, there is that small voice constantly telling you that it will not last. When you go to the doctor and they state that you have cancer and that they feel chemotherapy will prolong your life, Jezebel is there to remind you that many have not survived the treatments. When your unfaithful spouse turns his or her life over to the Lord, there is that voice constantly reminding you of all that he or she has done. Also, it is when the Lord makes a way for you to go back to college at your age and that small voice is there telling you that you are too old and that you will not make it. These are voices of Jezebel constantly taunting you and causing you to doubt that your God is bigger than your problems.

The key to your faith is your belief that through Christ all things are possible. You have to trust that if He has promised you something, then it is a promise that He must keep. Jezebel's voice may sometimes send you running to the cave, but trust that you have a God whose voice can bring you out every time. He can bring you out very easily if you know His voice. Remember, His sheep know His voice and to a stranger they will not answer. Are you in the cave today running from Jezebel's voice? If so, trust in the voice of the one and only Risen Savior to get you out.

In order that you might live a long life you've got to speak life into that which appears to be dead. When something in your life appears hopeless, turn to the One who can make it hopeful. It does not matter what Jezebel may say to you, be it big or small, your God really does care. Through His word He is speaking things down into your spirit that you need to use to combat the voice of Jezebel. Speak out of your belly what the Lord has deposited, rebuke the devil and he will have to flee.

So today I say silence Jezebel's voice. Let her know that her trickery will no longer work on you. Remind her of the God that you serve. Remind her that if God could part the Red Sea, and if God could allow David to slay Goliath, and if God could allow Daniel to come out of the lion's den, and if Jesus could wake Lazarus from the grave, and if Jesus could touch the casket at a funeral procession and wake a dead person, that nothing is too hard for your God. The Cross represents for each of us the Lord leaving His Holy Spirit to dwell within each of us. Therefore, when Jezebel speaks, we have a force so powerful that she can be silenced. So boldly go forward silencing Jezebel because with Christ you already have the VICTORY!

# STARTING MY DAY IN HIS PRESENCE

*You will show me the path of life; In Your presence is fullness of joy; At your right hand are pleasures forevermore.*

*Psalms 16:11*

I will be the first person to admit that I am not a morning person. It usually takes me a while to really get going in the mornings. Though I am not the most chipper person at 6:00 a.m., I do make sure that I start my day in His presence.

I've come to realize that if I start and end my day in the same manner, then I am able to pick up whatever needs to be picked up in the morning, and I am able to leave whatever needs to be left at night. By starting my day with God I am able to take time each morning and thank Him just for waking me up. Though He continually bestows His grace upon me throughout the day, I first begin by acknowledging Him. It is not that I spend a long time in the morning talking with Him. It depends on what we need to talk about which determines the length of time. All He asks is that you acknowledge Him. You may not do it the way that I do it, but make sure you talk with Him, it could change your entire attitude for the day.

I've come to learn that if I invite God in early each day, then throughout the day I can feel God's presence. You can feel His presence when a co-worker irritates you because you know that it is He who tames your tongue. When your spouse acts a little crazy in the mornings, remember to invite God into the presence of both of your lives because a family that prays together should remain on one accord. You can feel God's presence as you sit in the traffic on the way to work, or when someone cuts you off. Words that you once would have said now come out as blessings instead. Invite God in to all that you do...

Isn't it funny how we schedule our lives so much, but we forget to pencil God in? We can get up and get to work on time, yet forget to thank the One who allows us to wake each day. We praise ourselves for being on time to our job because we get our paychecks, but we forget that God has allowed us an even bigger check and that is a chance to spend eternity with Him. Just remember as you pull out your daily planners, your Outlook scheduler, handheld organizers, or whatever you use to organize yourself, pencil God in. Make sure that just as everyone else receives there time from you, make sure that God receives His time as well.

So if you did not begin your day in His presence, it's never too late. You will realize that there is fullness of joy in His presence. Situations that you would normally handle in a negative way, then begin to take on a different light when you start your day with Him. He will begin to show you how your faithfulness brings about pleasures forevermore. If you haven't tried beginning your day on your knees, give it a try. You will realize that it is not the quantity of time in His presence that matters, but it is the quality of time. So start your day over in His presence and challenge yourself to begin the rest of your days in His presence and see if you don't see a different result in your life.

# IN THE GARDEN WITH JESUS

*If, because of one man's trespass, death reigned through that one man, much more will those who receive the abundance of grace and the free gift of righteousness reign in life through the one man Jesus Christ.*

*Romans 5:17*

There are many gardens mentioned in the Bible, but there are two gardens that hold significant meaning in all of our lives. These two gardens are the Garden of Eden and the Garden of Gethsema'ne. It was in the Garden of Eden that Adam caused sin, but it was in the Garden of Gethsema'ne that Christ gave His life for our sins. Do you ever go into the garden with Jesus?

There is a great deal of significance placed on gardens today. Most people tend to work in their flowering gardens in order for their flowers to bloom and have life. Do you realize that you can go into your own garden with Jesus and He can flower your mind and heart so that they too can bloom? You see your garden with Jesus can be anywhere. It is that one place that you can go and only Jesus can reach you. It is in this place that you can find rest. It is in this place that you can be renewed. It is in this place that you can lay down all your cares.

I want to focus on the Garden of Gethsema'ne because this was the place that they arrested Jesus. This was the place that He was betrayed. This was the place that He chose to fulfill the scriptures. This was the place that God showed us His mercy because He didn't have to do it. God did not have to allow my precious Jesus to get up on the Cross. He wanted to show each of us that our sins could be blocked out in the same place that they started. Don't be fooled into thinking that God does not have a master plan. Ask yourself why did sin start in the garden and end in the garden? So truly sit back and think about the significance of a garden in your life. Make room for Jesus. Find the quality time. You make time to go to work, why not make time to go to your garden with Jesus?

This message is twofold. It is supposed to remind each of us that we need to find our own special garden with Jesus so that our relationship with Him can bloom. It also is to begin to show us how God's master plan works. You see many of us don't always look at the big picture. We don't bother to see past our today. But we serve a God who could look down into the ages and see that His son would have to restore man in the same place that man had fallen. *So* when you begin to look at your life, try to see past today. Know that the storms of life are but a temporary situation and that God has offered you a special garden where you and He can meet anytime you would like to. So begin to make a decision about spending time in the garden with Jesus.

# IS MY PRAYING IN VAIN?

*Be anxious for nothing, but in everything by prayer and supplication, with thanksgiving, let your requests be made known to God; and the peace of God, which surpasses all understanding, will guard your hearts and minds through Christ Jesus.*

*Philippians 4:6-7*

As I sit here pondering my life, I have to ask myself, "How many times have I wondered if my praying was in vain?"

Looking back, the obvious answer is no, of course not. Looking back is easy, but going through the trial is not always an easy task.

I've come today to offer biblical miracles to show how your praying is never in vain.

Look at the man who sat by the pool in Bethesda. He sat next to the pool for 38 years because legend had it that the angels would come during a season and bless all who were in the pool. The man's fervent prayers evoked more than an angel, they evoked Jesus to stop by.

Look at the lady with the issue of blood. She had prayed for 12 years for healing. Then one day she heard that Jesus was stopping by the temple, and she knew all that it would take would be healing from the hem of His garment. She not only got healing for her issue, but she was made whole. Will thou be made whole?

Look at Hannah who had a loving husband and a loving relationship, but was unable to conceive a child. Though her relationship with her spouse was admirable, this did not stop the desire of wanting a child. Hannah's prayers were so heartfelt, and her pledge to give that child back to God was so sincere, that God honored her bold and decisive act.

Though these are biblical stories, many of us can relate to having to wait on our prayers being answered. We all know that God does not work on our schedule because He knows your future and He therefore has His own schedule.

So today, I say remember and never forget that your praying is never in vain. God does hear you. God does know what's best for you. He knows that everything that He does is good and therefore there are times when a delay is necessary. So don't feel that just because you've asked God and He has not answered yet, that your praying is in vain. Trust that He knows both your wants and your needs in life and He is sufficient to decide which are best for you right now. So hold on because God is on the throne and all is right in the heavens.

# FORGIVING THE PAST

*And he touched my mouth, and said: "Behold, this has touched your lips; your guilt is taken away, and your sin forgiven."*

*Isaiah 6:7*

During my days as a social worker, I can remember many people who had current issues based on past experiences. This is true for most people. Though many seek total happiness, it always seems to slip through their hands because of the past. Many have tried to forget the past instead of learning to forgive the past.

I have talked to women who have been raped and molested. There is so much anger inside. If one is filled with anger, where is the room for God to step in and heal? The healing process must first begin with each of us. No, it is not fair that someone did horrible things to you, but you will never get past the hurt until you forgive.

Forgiving is easy to say, but hard to do. Forgiving requires praying for yourself as well as the person who inflicted the pain. The prayer that you say for that person might possibly save someone else from being victimized.

Remember, in John 4 the story of the Samaritan lady at the well. When she met Jesus at the well, He told her to drink from water that would cause her to thirst no more. Jesus told her all about her past. He told her about the married men that she had slept with. He told her about the current married man that she was sleeping with. But because of His love for us He offered her forgiveness. He offered her the forgiveness of her past. Has your past been forgiven?

This is what we have to do. I know that it is not easy. How can you move forward with the heavy baggage of the past? If your parents weren't good parents, forgive them anyway. If you got pregnant at a young age and your life has taken on a totally different path than you would have chosen, forgive yourself and move on.

Forgiving is about being able to move on in life by forgiving both yourself and the other person or situation. God has much work for you to do. God allowed you to go through what you've gone through in life because He knew you could handle it. Many would not have survived, but even in the midst He held your hand as you lived through the past. So now it is time to let go. Forgive everyone and everything because the past is gone. And it can never be replayed in the exact same manner. Trust God to lead the way going forward.

So today, as you begin to work on forgiving the past, remember that God loves you. He will be there to help you cry as you deal with the last remnants of the past hurt. Remember, weeping may endure for the night, but joy does come in the morning. Just trust that even though you can't see Him with your eyes, you can feel Him with your heart and know that He is there for you!

# HOW WELL DO YOU LISTEN?

*So then, my beloved brethren, let every man be swift to hear, slow to speak, slow to wrath; for the wrath of man does not produce the righteousness of God.*

*James 1:19-20*

As we mature in Christ, listening becomes more important than it has ever been in our lives.

It is when we are quiet that God begins to truly speak to our hearts.

It is then that we begin to understand why we had to go through all of the things that life has dealt us.

Some feel that they have been dealt a bad hand. I challenge you to say that God gave you what you could handle. Many would have been crushed, but you are still standing. Praise God.

There are times when marriages or relationships are in trouble because one person is so busy speaking, that they fail to listen to what their mate is saying. If your relationship is in trouble, stop talking and start listening. Listen to your mate. Listen to God. Stop listening to the world. The world will steer you wrong every time. No two people are exactly the same and therefore, no two relationships are exactly the same. If the two of you put God in the middle and listen to what He has to say, I promise that He will speak.

When your children are acting as if they have lost their minds and are continuing to get into one bad situation after the next, ask God how to handle it. Just as He knows you, He also knows your child. Every child is both different and unique. God has given you the task to *train them up in the way that they should go and when he is old, he shall not depart.* God is holding you accountable for giving them a firm Christian foundation. Trust Him to do the rest.

101

I have found in my life, that the older that I have become, the more I have begun to listen. I found that God has ordered my steps. I started out as a social worker, developing my listening skills. I then went to Corporate America to become a manager, same social work concept, different atmosphere. But now the charge has become different, I am still in Corporate America, but now God has me listening so that He can speak through me to people about the destination of their souls. I talk to people on a daily basis and try to encourage them to do the right thing and totally live their life for Christ. God is not impressed with your looks. He is impressed with the direction of your soul. It is at this point that I am most happy because collecting souls for Christ outweighs collecting dollars for Corporate America any day.

So stop talking to God and start listening to Him. Sit quietly and reflect on life, where you started and where you are now. You know that the best is yet to come, but it is all determined by how well you listen.

# THE TEARS THAT WILL NOT FALL

*Thus says the LORD: "Keep your voice from weeping, and your eyes from tears; for your work shall be rewarded, says the LORD, and they shall come back from the land of the enemy.*

*Jeremiah 31:16*

There are many of us that are the pillar of strength for all of our family and friends. We spend most of our lives making sure that everybody else is OK. Who do we turn to when our foundation appears to be shaky? Who do we call on when we have tears that will not fall?

Sometimes it seems just as much a curse as it does a blessing to be strong-willed, but trust God that it is a blessing. Everyone seems to pull on you from every direction. They never stop and wonder if you, the mighty one, ever get tired. They never stop and wonder how you make it through. They never stop and wonder...

If you are a person that has always been there for everybody else, know that God has been there for you. Those days when you wondered if you could go on, He blew His breath toward you and added strength unto you. He knows...

He knows of the times that you have been hurt, but you continued to press on. He knows of the times when others have disappointed you, but you continued to press on. He knows of the times when you have given selflessly of yourself as you continued to press on. He knows of the unshed tears that will not fall.

Know that God knows each of us individually. He designed you so that you could handle it all. He has put enough in you, so that when you become seriously tired, you know how to slip away into your private garden with Him. In this place those tears can fall. He will be there to catch them.

Each of your tears continually reminds Him that Job wasn't His only faithful servant. Trust that He knows how much you can bear. So if it looks like you've got too much, then know that He'll move some things around so that you can move on, all you have to do is ask.

So today, if it appears that life is getting to be too much, then call on the name of Jesus. It is through His name that you will receive your help. While you are a pillar of strength for your family, stay strong in your faith because God will be your pillar of strength. When situations look impossible, trust the God of Impossibility. When the storms are raging, know that He is your lighthouse. And know that God's hand is held out in front of you for those tears that will not fall just in case they ever do. Trust God!

# IF I COULD CRY YOUR TEARS

*As I remember your tears, I long night and day to see you, that I may be filled with joy.*

**2 Timothy 1:4**

One of the burdens that we carry as a child of God is that we always wanting to help others through their storms. Always wanting to ease someone else's pain away. If I could cry your tears?

As I look at many Christians today, sometimes the pain of life is evident on their face and even more evident as you engage in conversation. Though many try hard to hide what is going on inside, some things God will show you through your Holy Vision. As you talk with people about the things that are going on in their life, do you ever wonder why God allowed them to go through that which they are going through? Is it always for the person to learn a lesson alone, or does He purposely set your appointed time to meet that person so that you can bear their pain? You see, God knows what we can and cannot handle. He knows that which is breaking someone else down can easily be turned around when turned over to you. Remember, He knows your strengths and your weaknesses. If you are about His business then He will be about yours.

Do you understand why God allows certain things to happen the way that they do? Unfortunately, none of us can truly answer this question, but those of us who know God, know that it wasn't by mistake. We know that though good and bad both happen, God is there with us through it all. He knows the decisions that we will make, He knows the disappointments that we will give Him and this is why He allows others to bear some of the burdens. He knows that there are some situations that some truly handle better than others. He knows that some things that makes one person cry, makes others wish to cry for them because their outlook on that particular subject is stronger.

When it would appear that one lesson is to be learned, do you ever look back and realize that there were more lessons to be learned? As you bear the burden of wanting to cry someone else's tears, do so knowing that God has ordered your steps. Do so knowing that He appointed you to be the head and not the tail. Do so knowing that if you could cry their tears then you would show them that joy does come in the morning.

So today, when you bear the burden of someone else's pain, do so knowing that God appointed you to do so. He appointed you so that a certain testimony could come forth. You see everything in life has a purpose and if I could cry your tears I would erase the pain. But, because we serve the True and Risen Savior, then we know that we can cast our cares upon Him and He will cry our tears.

# GIVE IT UP, TURN IT LOOSE

*But God will redeem my soul from the power of the grave, for He shall receive me.*

**Psalms 49:15**

How many nights have you stayed awake worrying about a problem, a family member, finances, health related issues, or some other very important matter? Did you have an answer in the morning, or were you just tired?

I come today to say "give it up, turn it loose." You serve a God that never sleeps nor slumbers.

As Christians we sometimes take on battles that our physical being will never win. We sometimes feel that God is moving too slowly to work out the situation, so we stay up all night worrying. Depending upon the severity of the situation, we sometimes spend all night crying.

Why?

Do you not serve a God who is strong and mighty?

Do you not serve a God who is able to work out every situation?

Do you not understand that if God could go into the death realm and bring Lazarus back to life, then surely your problem can't be that bad?

What about Job? He lost everything he had. Yet he said, "I will trust the Lord". Follow his example. Trust the Lord.

*"Remember weeping may endure for a night, but joy cometh in the morning".*

Stop spending your nights worrying about your problems.

Pray. Give it up, turn it loose. He is waiting. You serve a God who knows just how much you can handle.

# SWEEPING THE HOUSE

*Thus also faith by itself, if it does not have works, is dead.*

*James 2:17*

Is your body the temple of God? Does Christ reside in you? If so, are there some things inside of your house that need to be swept?

Many of us spend each day talking about things that we know we need to do, but for some reason we just haven't done them.

Many of us are living with someone out of wedlock, fornicating, or committing adultery, yet we continue to profess how much we love Christ, but then are forced to squirm in our seats when the Pastor teaches on these subjects.

How about those of us that have promised Christ on many occasions that we would stop doing that which we know is wrong, yet we continue to go to ask for forgiveness yet again?

How about those of us who say that the past is behind us, yet we silently cry about our past when no one is watching?

I come today to say to you "Sweep the House." *Faith without works is dead.* It is not enough to say that you have changed, or to say that you are sorry, or to say that the past is the past. Put your words into action.

The tongue is a very powerful weapon, yet it is just mere talk if what is said is not backed up.

God is waiting for us to "Sweep the House." Look at the lady at the well. Did Jesus not know that she had been with many men? Didn't He still heal her of her past? Didn't He think her worthy, so much so, that He met her at an appointed destination? Can't He do the same for you?

If there are some things in your life, that require the assistance of God, just ask. I promise that you will never be displeased with the final outcome. You might be uncomfortable in-between as He breaks you down, but what a blessing as He builds you back up.

So today, I say, stop talking about what you need to do to "Sweep the House," and just do it. God will be pleased.

# WHERE IS YOUR FAITH?

*But He said to them, "Why are you so fearful? How is it that you have no faith?"*

*Mark 4:40*

What is your definition of faith?

My definition of faith is stepping out into the unknown, knowing that if God does not give you a platform to stand on, He will give you wings to fly.

Faith is a difficult concept to grasp, unless you have truly come to know Christ for yourself.

Faith often times means stepping out of your comfort zone. Examples of comfort zones are long term relationships that are going nowhere, dead-end jobs that no longer challenge you, living from paycheck to paycheck, or perhaps never going after your life-long dreams.

Examine your comfort zones. Is this truly a good zone for you? Life has much to offer, if only we would use Godly Wisdom. The doors would be open.

God's blueprint for each of the lives of His children is magnificent. If God told you that He was going to work out your situation, then believe it. Remember, God cannot and does not tell a lie.

If Jesus could make the winds and waves obey...
If Jesus could feed more than 5000 people with 2 fish and 5 loaves of bread...
If Jesus could wake Lazarus from the grave...

If Jesus could...

Jesus can, and Jesus does exactly what He has promised.

111

The question becomes, do you have the faith to believe that He can do the impossible in your life?

## MUSTARD SEED FAITH

*So Jesus said to them, "Because of your unbelief; for assuredly, I say to you, if you have faith as a mustard seed, you will say to this mountain, "Move from here to there," and it will move, and nothing will be impossible for you.*

**Matthew 17:20**

Life brings storms into each of our lives that require the faith of a mustard seed.

When it seems that there is no way out of the storm, Jesus is standing by asking us to call on Him.

Calling on Him is not enough you have to believe He can do that which He says that He will do. Remember, Jesus did not perform any miracles during His walk on earth to a person with unbelief. You have to believe and confess, "It is so."

If you are in the midst of your storm, step back and go into your prayer closet and worship God.

It is when we are weak, that He is strong. It is the "mustard seed" faith that stirs God.

Look at the Gentile lady in Matthew 15:21-28. It was her "mustard seed" faith that moved Jesus. This woman's daughter was possessed with demons and she cried out to Jesus for help. The apostles urged Jesus to send her away, but Jesus spoke to her and explained that it was not the appointed time to come to the house of the Gentiles. Yet she continued to worship Him. Jesus acknowledged her faith, so much so, that He answered her prayer before her appointed time.

This is the same thing that your faith can do. If you've been laid off, worship God because if He closes a door, then He'll open a window. Just hold steady to your faith. Know that

God is listening. Take time to find out where He wants you to go next. Remember, a job is not just a place to earn your paycheck it is your place to minister to all who are lost. So step back and allow God to use you.

Always remember and never forget, if God brought you to the storm, surely He can bring you through the storm. All it takes is your little "mustard seed" faith.

# STRUGGLES CAN BE HIS WILL

*Now no chastening seems to be joyful for the present, but painful; nevertheless, afterward it yields the peaceable fruit of righteousness to those who have been trained by it.*

**Hebrews 12:11**

As Christians we often associate struggling with the enemy, but what if I say that struggles are sometimes the Will of God?

Difficulties come to everybody, but they can be easier to bear if we look at them as meaningful. Christ's suffering accomplished salvation for all who believe. The Savior, who suffered, will not lead His followers into meaningless trials.

Struggles and suffering are forms of disciplinary actions that help build our character. These types of disciplinary actions show God's love and it is always for the good of the child, producing the character of "righteousness."

I often get into conversations about finances, budgeting, investing or some related topic, and almost every time in this conversation, the person will make the statement that if God only gave them a certain amount of money then they would be OK going forward. My normal comeback is, if God can't trust you with $200 why would He trust you with $200,000?

Living from paycheck to paycheck is a reality for many people. Not knowing how to manage their finances is a reality as well. Many disagree that they can't manage their finances they usually state that they just don't make enough, yet most of us got a pay increase last year, correct? Are you taking the amount of your increase and investing it or saving it? Last year you seemed to have managed on the amount that you were making, so why not continue budgeting your money on that amount? Put the extra money into some type of interest bearing savings,

CD, money market, savings bond, etc. Save something for a rainy day, because just as sure as God is God, He will allow some rainy days to come your way to point out your lack of discipline. Remember, you have to be faithful over a few things before He can make you ruler over many.

I said all of this to say that God will allow you to struggle in your finances until you learn some discipline. Discipline sometimes means not seeing every movie that comes out, or eating chicken instead of steak or drinking tap water, rather than bottled water. Sometimes it is the little things that add up.

I've often stated that you pay God first, yourself second, and everybody and everything else next. This still holds true. Sowing into the Kingdom of God is very important. Why should He be faithful to you, when you are not faithful to Him?

Remember, anything and everything that we go through are tests, tests to see who will endure to the end. Your struggles may get rough and even bend you a little, but by the Grace of God they cannot break you, if you put your trust in Him.

# WHO TOUCHED ME?

*And Jesus immediately knowing in Himself that power had gone out of Him, turned around in the crowd and said, "Who touched My clothes?"*

*Mark 5:30*

Did you know that if you stood in a crowd of millions of people, God could still pick you out when you reached out and touched Him?

When you are in situations where you see no hope, know that God is the hope that you are looking for. God is the One who can mess up the checks at the bank and allow that check that should have bounced to be paid. God is the One who can touch your sick child in the midnight hours and that child awake in the morning, as if nothing was ever wrong. God is the One who will give you an increase in pay, when the company has announced a freeze in annual reviews. But this kind of grace comes from reaching out and touching the hem of His garment.

In Mark 5:25-32 there is a woman who had an issue of blood for 12 years. This woman knew that if she could only touch His garments, that she would be made whole. What she did not count on was Jesus detecting her touch in a crowd so large. But I come to remind everyone of just how awesome He really is.

This woman's faith, in just a touch of His garment, caused her to receive a fourfold response from Jesus:

He called her daughter
He assured her that her body was healed through her faith
He sent her away free from all anxiety
He healed her

Therefore, if you think that God does not see you, I beg to differ? He does. If you call on Him, then He'll answer. If you seek Him, you'll find Him. If you knock, the doors will be opened.

So, whatever the problem you are facing today, reach out and touch the hem of His garment. Your problem may be of lesser concerns by human measurement, but not by Christ. He stops for everyone. Just be prepared, when He stops, for Him to ask you "Who Touched Me?" Remember, the power of a touch.

# PRIVATE STRUGGLES, PUBLIC VICTORIES

*For whatsoever is born of God overcometh the world: and this is the victory that overcometh the world, even our faith.*

**1 John 5:4**

Have you ever noticed that no matter what some people may be going through, they continually praise God? These are the people who have come to understand that God will allow private struggles, yet public victories.

In order to warrant this from God, you've got to be faithful. You've got to understand that no matter what you are going through you must stand on the Word of God. You've got to know that beyond a shadow of a doubt, God will do exactly what He said He would. You have got to believe.

God will take a woman with an unfaithful spouse and still allow that person to minister to someone who is going through the exact same thing. This woman will be able to stand boldly before God because in Him lies her trust.

God will allow a person without a job to minister to someone who is complaining about their job. God knows that this person has come to a place in their life when they have stood and declared that without God they are nobody. It is He who supplies their needs.

Struggles are difficult. It is in this valley where you are asking God, why me? It should be in this valley that you are waiting on His reply of why not you? God needs to be able to trust you with the understanding that He is God. Before Him there is no other. If He can't do it, then it can't be done.

God needs all of His faith-walkers to know that He is the only person that you have to tell everything that you are going through. Stop telling the world, they only continue to judge. Allow God to be your Best Friend. I promise that no one else can keep a secret like Him. He is the only one worthy of your continued praise.

So today, as you face your new challenges, boldly go forth speaking the Word of God. It is not always the final results of the test that count. It is sometimes the way you get to the final results that becomes the testimony.

# WHEN THE SUN REFUSES TO SHINE

*From the rising of the sun to its setting the name of the LORD is to be praised!*

*Psalms 113:3*

It has often been said that age is nothing but a number, this is true in many cases, but far from the truth in others. As you walk with Christ for many years, your age becomes much more than a number. Your age hopefully directly correlates with your maturity in Christ. As you get older and more mature, you truly have days when the sun refuses to shine. The question here becomes how do you handle it?

Do you allow all of the situations in your life to stand in the way of the many other blessings that God has in store for you? Do you sit back and have a pity party pointing out all of the things that are going wrong? Do you let the devil in?

As we mature in Christ, we should become more seasoned Saints. This means that we get to a point where we stop running here and there expecting everyone to pray for us, and develop our own personal relationship with the Father to pray for ourselves. There is very strong power in prayer. God does hear the prayers of the righteous.

All of us have situations in our lives that we are not pleased with. The issue becomes how do we handle them? I could spend my time worrying about the situation or I can worship God more for the situations that He has already worked out. Just think back to last year, you had issues then that now seem so long ago. This is the same thing that will happen with your current issues when you take them to the altar and leave them there.

Word of caution - If you take it to the altar, leave it there!! Wait on God for an answer, but while you are waiting begin to focus on the positives. If nothing else needs to be said just think about how far He has brought you. I can't speak for anyone else, but I know all of the things that Sheila has done, and I thank God for forgiving me.

On those cloudy days think about the days when the sun has shone brightly. The object is to worship God in the good times and in the bad because either way He is worthy to be praised. He woke you up this morning. He started you on your way. He kept you from dangers seen and unseen. Need I say more?

When the sun refuses to shine, speak to the mountain that is clouding your path and tell it to move. Cast it into the sea. Remember, the sun will rise each and every day, the question becomes will you see it with your natural eyes or with your spiritual eyes? The answer does make a difference.

# YOU KNOW THAT YOU KNOW

*Now we know that you know all things, and need none to question you; by this we believe that you came from God.*

*John 16:30*

Many of us know God when things are going well. What about those other days? On those days when the sun refuses to shine, do you still trust Him? When the devil is hitting you with everything that he's got, do you know that you know in whom you trust?

Many people would tell you that they know in whom they trust, but do they really know when things get rough? Oh it's easy to praise God when things are going well, but what about during those trying seasons? Do you know that you know in whom you trust when you lose a child, when your marriage fails, when you find out you are HIV positive, or when you find out you have cancer? Do you know?

I've had a chance to talk to women who miscarried a child and they sometimes blame God for their loss? This same person prior to the tragedy in their life would have sworn that they knew whom they knew. It's sometimes very difficult to hold your tongue because you want to explain to the person how God is still blessing them in spite of all that they are going through. But my days as a social worker taught me that sometimes it is best to listen as a person grieves and allow a shoulder instead of advice. Some situations only God can resolve. Know that He will never leave you.

I've had a chance to talk with people who are HIV positive, yet their faith is strong. Many of them will be the first to tell you that initially they were angry with God. Many felt that they had lived a righteous life, yet they felt they were being punished. Prior to finding out the doctor's diagnosis their faith was strong. It wasn't until their grieving period ended and they allowed God to minister to their heart that their faith resurfaced. Know that He will never leave you.

Both tragedies and real-life trauma can sometimes shake the faith of the holiest of us. It is during these times that we have to remember that our trials do not come to break us down they come to build us up. You see, God allows things to happen to those who can handle it. Know that He does not allow you to go to a storm that He cannot bring you through. All tests someday become testimonies.

So as you go before the Lord today, go with confidence that you know whom you know. Let Him know that *though they slay me, yet will I trust you.*" You see God is still God. His Word always holds true. Trust God to be your beacon of light during those dark times in your life. No storm lasts forever. Seasons come and go, but throughout it all God remains the same.

# IT'S JUST A HOLDING PATTERN

*Follow the pattern of the sound words which you have heard from me, in the faith and love which are in Christ Jesus.*

*2 Timothy 1:13*

Does it sometimes appear that you just keep going around in circles? It is as if you can see the blessing in front of you, but you just cannot quite reach it. Is it possible that God has you in a holding pattern?

When we think of a holding pattern, the first thing that usually comes to mind is an airplane. When the airplane is trying to land and it is unable to land due to issues communicated by the control tower it is in a holding pattern. It might be that there are other planes in front of it and it must wait its turn or it might be that the weather outside is too bad to land just yet, so you have to circle the airport until the storm passes over.

As we take and relate this back to many of our lives we might find that God has us in holding patterns. We find that we are just like Jonah and that God has taken us into the belly of the fish to talk to us. We are so accustomed to talking to people, that we sometimes become confused when God takes us into the belly of the fish to block out the noise. Unfortunately, many times in life, our friends become noise to us. God will put us in positions of solitude when He wants complete quiet from us so that we listen to Him only. Trust that one-way or another God will be heard.

When the airplane is in the air and cannot land because it has to wait on others to land first, this is sometimes God's way of making us wait for our blessing. Many times we miss our blessing because we wanted it right then and did not want to wait for God's answer. We want a new job right now, so God allows us to have a job because it is the desire of our hearts, but it is not necessarily the one that He was working out for us. We want that particular man or woman right now, so God allows us to have him or her, God did not put the marriage together, we did. We want to put our children on the altar, but they do not appear to change, simply because God has to change us first. Begin to recognize the holding patterns. Don't become discouraged because all holding patterns have a purpose, a plan and a process. Take this time to become quiet and listen to what the Master has to say.

It is when storms are raging in our lives that many of us turn to God. We've prayed that our loved ones will turn their lives over to Christ, but they haven't. We've prayed that we will get our finances straightened out, but we haven't. We have infirmities in our bodies, yet God has not healed us. We've prayed without ceasing, yet our prayers seem to go unanswered. This is a holding pattern. Know that God will always answer His children in His own time. He sometimes answers with a yes and sometimes with a no, but always with an answer. The answer does not necessarily come in the package that we always want to see, but with our spiritual eyes we still know that it is God answering. Please understand that God has to take you through a process. Waiting is one of the highest orders of discipline in the body of Christ. It is during our waiting period that we should concentrate on worshiping God because through it all He is still worthy.

So today, as you examine your life, begin to look at it with your spiritual eyes. Are there some situations where God has you in a holding pattern? If so know that they don't last always. All holding patterns have a purpose, a plan, and a process. Don't try to bypass the steps; otherwise you will see it again. Remember when tests are put before you and you fail due to your disobedience or lack of understanding, know that you will see it again. Trust that God has a master plan and all that He allows is for your good. Trust and believe that whatever holding pattern you are in that He will work it out.

# DO THE SMALL THINGS REALLY MATTER TO GOD?

*...is it too small a thing for you that the God of Israel has separated you from the congregation of Israel, to bring you near to himself, to do service in the tabernacle of the LORD, and to stand before the congregation to minister to them;*

**Numbers 16:9**

There are many of us who face problems that seem insurmountable and we gladly turn them over to God. There are some problems that are small that we try to fix ourselves. I've come today to ask, "Do the small things really matter to God?"

Those small issues in our lives are just as important as the large issues. God wants to handle those as well. He wants us all to know that the small things really do matter to Him.

You see God is concerned with all of us. Not just the parts that we choose to hand over to Him, but all that we go through. Because He is a just God, He does allow us to try to fix our problems and He also allows us to turn them over to Him, but it is our choice. Where many of us run into trouble is when we hold on to the small issues so long that they become big issues.

The Lord has stated in His Word to cast our cares upon Him. There are many people who feel that God is not one who should be bothered with the small stuff. Well, if we gave all of our cares to Him, then we would have more time to do His ministry. We would have more time to worship Him. We would have more time to come into His presence with a clear mind and heart. We would not have to stay up at night worrying because He would stay up working it out. We would not have to cry when the small stuff turns into big stuff because God would have stopped that before it ever happened.

So today, when you have to make small decisions, ask our Big God. He will direct whether you should buy that new car right now. He will direct whether you should move into that new apartment or stay where you are. He will direct you where to shop more efficiently for your family. There are small things in our lives that we never think to take to God until it becomes a problem. On a daily basis we should be spending quiet time in His presence, this is the place where you cast it all upon Him. So do the small things really matter to God? Absolutely. Trust that your little problems put before our Big God will be resolved in no time.

# DO YOU REALLY KNOW HIM?

*Even the Spirit of truth, whom the world cannot receive, because it neither sees him nor knows him; you know him, for he dwells with you, and will be in you.*

*John 14:17*

Look within yourself and ask the question: Do I really know Him?

It seems that as things are going well in our life many of us feel that we truly know the Lord. When things get a little rough or we hit a major storm, we begin to question if He really loves us. Many of us fail to realize that God is God and He does not change.

In His word He has never promised that there would not be cloudy days, as a matter of fact He guarantees them. He has guaranteed that some days there will be sunshine and other days there will be rain, but your strength in the "faith walk" is determined by your belief in Him. Your faith that believes through Christ all things are possible.

Knowing God means knowing that some things are worth working hard for. Getting to know God requires time and attention. It requires cultivating your relationship with Him. It requires agape love. But, can you achieve these things if you do not believe that through Him all things are possible? I am not talking about the kind of knowing Him where you praise God on Sundays and then forget Him for the rest of the week. I am talking about spending time in God's presence. It is only in His presence that you really begin to know who He really is and what He wants for you in life.

Knowing God means knowing that because you are His sheep then you know His voice. There are times when some of us get confused when the devil tells us something because we think that it is the Lord. If you begin to read His Word and accept it into your heart, you will begin to know

Him and His voice. Don't be lead astray because you did not know who spoke to you. Walk with Him as you talk with Him.

I spend a lot of time talking about developing a relationship with God because it is very important in your walk with Him. It would be a shame to walk with the Lord, yet never know Him. Even though it is only one of Him, there is more than enough of Him that He will take the time to talk with you personally. All it takes is for you to begin by calling on His name. There is no other name that brings peace to your soul than that of Jesus. So talk with Him today and ask Him how you can really get to know Him because it is a relationship that you will come to cherish once you start.

# WALKING ON WATER

*And Peter answered him, "Lord, if it is you, bid me come to you on the water." He said, "Come." So Peter got out of the boat and walked on the water and came to Jesus.*

*Matthew 14:28-29*

Walking on water requires faith. Many of us read this passage and focus only on literally walking on water, but there are some things that God is calling us to do that require that we walk on water in our faith.

Walking on water can be anything in your life that you are afraid to do. It can be deciding to go back to college. It can be deciding to start your own business. It can be deciding to write a book. It can be deciding to answer the call on your life. It can be deciding to be a financial advisor. It can be deciding to have the unwanted child and not the abortion. It can be anything that requires your mustard seed faith. The faith that tells you that God will sustain you.

As you think about the things that God has told you to do, you sometimes become scared. Scared because God will surely call you to do something that requires that you step outside of your comfort zone. It requires that if you are going to achieve it, then you have to have complete faith in Him. The question becomes are you afraid to walk on water? Think about Peter as the Lord bid him to come, he was having great success until he began to doubt. Doubt is a back-breaker of God's Word. Doubt will cause you to believe that there is something or someone bigger than your God. Don't feed into the myth. God doesn't call the equipped, He equips the ones that He calls. So take that first step today.

As you begin to yield to the call on your life, God will continue to test your faith. The more you show faithfulness, the more He will ask of you. The more He tests you, the higher the level of your ministry becomes. He takes you from one level of glory to the next. He prepares you for the next steps. Trust me, He would not bid you to come unless He has already prepared you for the walk on water.

So today, give serious thought to walking on water. Remember, it requires your complete faith in Him. Your faith that shows God that you will not doubt Him. The faith that says that you will not look down to make sure that you are not sinking. The faith that says you will not look back. Walking on water requires looking ahead. Focusing only on the goal that God has put before you. So today, I ask, will you walk on water for God?

# HE'S ONLY A PRAYER AWAY

*A Prayer of David. Hear a just cause, O LORD; attend to my cry! Give ear to my prayer from lips free of deceit!*

*Psalms 17:1*

There are days when we allow our troubles to consume our every waking thought. As a matter of fact, some of us toss and turn at night and allow it to consume us then as well. We become so focused on our problems that we forget He's only a prayer away.

Many of us face trouble that we sometimes feel overwhelms us. We believe God can do abundantly above all that we may ask, but for other people and not ourselves. We spend a great deal of our time believing for everybody else. We trust God to see others through.

As we begin to get our lives in focus then we should realize that He's only a prayer away. If He can bless others, then know that He can do the same for you. He can give you a promotion on your job. He can increase your savings, or better yet, create you a savings. He can and will do it for you. It is through your prayers that you make your request known to Him. Nothing is too hard for God.

Some of us go down on bended knees and we pray earnestly, but then we get up with doubt in our heart. We feel that just because we prayed about something then it should come to pass. The part that we miss is that God saw our heart. He saw that though we prayed, we did not believe. God needs your mustard seed faith. The faith that says no matter what may come, you believe God and His precious promises. Even when it looks like the situation is going in the opposite direction of what we may want it to, we still stand on our faith that God is working it out.

So today, wipe away the tears and begin to focus on the fact that He's only a prayer away. Just as He answers the prayers of others, He will do the same for you. Just believe that God is the solution to all of your problems. As you go down on bended knees, stay there until you get your breakthrough. God is no respecter of persons therefore what He's done for others He will do the same for you. So remember, to do just as David to ask God to *hear a just cause, O LORD; attend to my cry! Give ear to my prayer from lips free of deceit!*

# HELP MY UNBELIEF

*Immediately the father of the child cried out and said, "I believe; help my unbelief!"*

*Mark 9:24*

I must begin by confessing that there have been times when I have put more trust in my fear, than I trusted God with the belief that He would see me through. Why is it we can trust God for those things that we know He will provide, but question other things? Today, I come asking the Father to help our unbelief.

Don't get me wrong, I praise the Lord on a daily basis, but there are times when we allow our fleshly fears to overrule our Spiritual promises. Most of us have never gone hungry, most of us have never lived on the street, most of us have all of our needs met, yet why do we walk around with fear in today's economy? Today's economy suggests that we should walk around on eggshells because pink slips are forth coming rapidly. Jobs we once thought to be secure no longer are secure. Is it possible God wants you to stand strong in your faith? If He has always supplied your needs, why wouldn't He continue to do so? Who do you serve, your job or your God? Who do you have faith in your job or your God?

There are times in life when God will allow a pink slip to push you to your next level. We become complacent in life and sometimes we need to be shook-up. We need to be shook-up to realize what is important. Many of us go to these jobs day-in and day-out, yet we find no joy. Eight plus hours is a long time to spend at a place that doesn't bring you joy. Look within yourself and find out what brings you joy. God has given all of us a gift. A gift that when used will bring about a richness. It might not be a financial richness, but surely it is a richness of the soul. When your spirit is happy everything else falls in line.

I am not writing this thought because I think that someone is going to receive a pink slip. I am writing because someone needs to remember that God provides for our needs. If He provided once, then He'll provide again. It is when we question our belief that He will see us through that brings about our unbelief. Remember, Jesus did not perform any miracles to those with unbelief. So believe that your God is bigger than your problems. Believe that your God has already predestined your victory. You just have to hold on to your belief to make it to the other side of your storm.

So today, when you become a little nervous or fear steps in, remember to ask the Father to help your unbelief. Ask Him to remove all doubt because through Christ all things are possible. Step forward with the faith that if He closes one door then surely you can look around the house and find another one open because He has promised, in His Word, to never leave you nor forsake you!

# ALL OF THE FAITH THAT I LET SLIP

*My steps have held fast to thy paths, my feet have not slipped.*

*Psalms 17:5*

Does your faith sometimes waiver? Sometimes you trust God completely and then other times you question if He will come to your rescue. Have you ever thought about the faith that you let slip?

Our faith slips when we allow doubt to rule our thinking rather than trust God to make a way. Our faith slips when it is time to pay our tithes and rent at the same time. Our faith slips when we receive that unexpected bill. Our faith slips when our promised check doesn't arrive on time. Our faith slips...

If you truly begin to think about all of the times that you have truly prayed, yet worried at the same time, you begin to get a better understanding of the faith that you let slip. Oh, part of you trusted God and part of you trusted the seed of doubt planted by the enemy. God said He would supply all of your needs, but you trusted that promise for others. Though you will never admit it aloud, you had more trust in the seed of doubt than you did in God's promises. This is a shame because your little seed of doubt blocked your blessing.

Have you ever wondered why God grants some things and not others? Could it be that there are some things that you truly turned over to Him and others that you gave Him and then turned around and picked back up? You see if you want God to work out the entire solution, then you have to give Him the entire problem. He is able to do exceedingly and abundantly above all that we may ask. That's the key. Ask and believe.

So today, make a conscious effort to make sure that your faith does not slip. When God promises you something, don't allow the seed of doubt to creep in. Cast it out. Remember, if God promises, then it shall come to pass. Remember, your faith in God determines your fortitude in God. So remember, and don't forget to always remind yourself that *my steps have held fast to thy paths, my feet have not slipped.*

# WHO WILL CATCH ME IF I FALL?

***...And Jesus said to Simon, "Do not be afraid. From now on you will catch men."***

*Luke 5:10*

The hardest thing about stepping out on faith is the fear of the unknown. Fear that if I were to fall then who would be there to catch me? Everyone wants to get to the finish line, but many find it hard to even start the race.

Think about fear and how it insinuates that God is not capable. The reason faith is the evidence of things not seen is because many would only step out because they have seen the end. But God wants our unconditional trust in all situations. He wants us to trust that He is God.

Faith is stepping out into the unknown with the belief that if God does not give you a platform to stand on, then He will give you wings to fly. This is a feeling that should get deep down into our spirits because God never fails.

Even when it looks like nothing is going to turn out right, God has a way of stepping into the situation and turning it around, just like that. So if He is telling you to step out on faith, then do it.

There are many people reading these thoughts that God is telling to step out on faith. He has told you to write the book. He has told you to start the ministry. He has told you to be the parent that your child needs. He has told you to start your own business. He has told you...

Turn it over to Him. Know that He will never leave you. Know that if He has told you to step out on faith then the path has already been cleared. Know that He has given you all that you need at this point in time to do what He has called you to do.

Remember that if He has called you to do something, *then He is the one to catch you when you fall*. He knows that we will stumble and sometimes fall along the way on this "faith walk," but know that He will send His heavenly angels to encamp around you, as well as many of His earthly angels. What God has already blessed must come to pass.

So have the *"courage to not follow where the path may lead...go instead where there is no path and leave a trail..."*

# ALPHA AND OMEGA
*"I am the Alpha and the Omega," says the Lord God, who is and who was and who is to come, the Almighty.*

*Revelation 1:8*

Knowing whom you are and what you are supposed to be doing in the Kingdom of God is very important. Understanding these things first begins with understanding that the Lord God is Alpha and Omega, the Beginning and the End.

As we grow in Christ, the calling upon our lives becomes clearer, if we are paying attention. God shows us, little by little, what we are called to do. As we study His Word He begins to deposit those things that are needed to equip us. As we begin to acknowledge that we are open and willing vessels, then He begins to use us.

One of the problems that we sometimes run into in our lives is, when God calls, we run in the opposite direction. We think that if we can go out into the world and do everything that we are big and bad enough to do then He will not want to use us. Wrong, if He has called you, then He's called you for a purpose. You can run, but you can't hide. He is God. There's no place that you can hide, that He cannot find you. So you can run until you get tired, or you can accept that God's Will shall be done in your life.

Another problem we sometimes face is that we only want to give part of ourselves. We are willing to be open vessels, but with limited use. We know that we are supposed to walk all of the way with God, but the future is scary so we only want to give a little of ourselves. We are not convinced that we are the right people for the job. Surely there are other people who speak more articulate than us? Surely there are others who's writing is always grammatically correct? Surely there are others who always know the right things to say and we don't? We realize everything wrong with us, but forget that God will still use us. He knows who we are and what we are capable of doing with Him as the head of our lives. We've got to stop trying to see with our natural vision and look with our Holy Vision. God does not make mistakes!

So today, as you step forward to the calling on your life, step forward knowing whose you are and what you are supposed to be doing. Step forward knowing that the Great I Am knows your beginning from your end. So hearken to that voice as He speaks to you and tells you what to do. Remember, He does not start something that He does not plan to finish. So if He has started a good work in you, then hang on in there as He completes what He started because "I am the Alpha and the Omega," says the Lord God, who is and who was and who is to come, the Almighty.

# BEFORE I KNEW YOU

*It was I who knew you in the wilderness, in the land of drought.*

*Hosea 13:5*

As I was driving home today, listening to the radio, a song came on and the young lady sang a song about how the devil can't stop me no matter how he tries. As I listened to this song I began to praise God. I had to praise God because even before I knew Him, He was there. As I wandered in the wilderness He was there.

As the song went off, I began to have worship service with the Lord. You see sometimes we forget where He brought us from. We forget that He had His hands on our lives long ago.

I thought back to all of the people that He's had in my life. Some good, some bad, but all to teach a life lesson. I thought back to my college days at FAMU and how many students were messing up in school, and how I had no choice but to succeed because I was the first from my mother's family to go to college. Though it was never stated, I felt I carried the hopes, prayers, and dreams of my entire family. I knew I could never let them down.

I had a grandmother who had expectations for my life. Thank God those expectations lined up with the Will of God. Some of her ways were very strict, some weren't. She was a woman of character and principles that she instilled in me. They all made me the better for who I am today.

I can remember being in college and getting baptized. I remember the look on her face as the tears ran down mine. It was then that she realized that God had truly heard her prayers. You see anyone can go to school, but it is the prayers of yourself and others that help you stay in school.

I must honestly say that I have not always done right. I have messed up and will probably mess up again, but because I am His, I can get up and start over again. So remember, today, as you look at life, do so knowing and understanding that even before you knew Him, He already knew you. He's just waiting on you to recognize Him and His purpose for your life.

# THERE IS A BLESSING

*Thus says the LORD: "As the wine is found in the cluster, and they say, 'Do not destroy it, for there is a blessing in it,' so I will do for my servants' sake, and not destroy them all.*

*Isaiah 65:8*

There are many Christians today who stand in the midst of a storm. A storm that at first glance would appear that it is going to destroy them. I've come today to say stand strong in your faith because there is a blessing on the other side of your storm.

There are many children of the Most High King who are in financial trouble today. There are many who have children that are out of control. There are many who are suffering persecution on their job. There are many who are suffering persecution in their ministry. Well, hold on because God is not through with you yet.

You see financial dilemmas do have resolutions. This statement probably doesn't sit well with many who are going through this dilemma, but know that there is help. There are bill consolidation programs. There are home equity loans. There are state agencies that help. Sometimes a second job is necessary to get you through this crunch. Sometimes wisdom is necessary when deciding what is a necessity and what is a luxury. There are times when a check will show up just like that. I don't know how each person has come to this point in life, but the reality is that you are here and something needs to be done. Ask the One who can help. Take it to God in prayer, but most importantly listen to His answer. Stand strong while in the midst of your storm because there is blessing on the other side of your storm.

For that child who is out of control try different methods. First, look within yourself to see your example then begin to evaluate the environment. We want to give our children all of the luxuries in life, and yet we forget to teach them how to earn it. There are times when you have to look outside of your household for help. They have programs such as Big Brother/Big Sister. Many of the churches have mentoring programs. Involve the children in community activities. Expose the child to all of the possibilities in life, not just the ones that they see from day to day. But in the midst of doing all that you can, do make sure that you take it to God first. Talk with Him in earnest about the concerns of your household and see what He offers because He will offer you some advice. So hang on in there because there is a blessing on the other side of your storm.

Persecution on the job and in your ministry can be very disheartening, but turn it over to God. If He has called you, then know that He knew all that you would go up against and He has prepared you. Stand firm on what He has told you to do. Perform on that job as if He is your Supervisor. Perform in that ministry as if you report directly to Him. Because remember in both of these situations, He is in control. When things get a little hectic, slip away into your quiet garden where He can rejuvenate so that you can go back into the fight. Stand strong and know that there is a blessing on the other side of your storm.

So today, as you ride out of your storm, know that God has His hand on you. He will never allow the storm to overtake you, when you have turned it over to Him. Know that He will be the light that directs you in the storm. Every time that it would appear that you are about to drown, child of God, know that He will throw you a life preserver. So hang on in there because storms don't last always, but tough people do.

## IT'S A SET-UP

***For the LORD of hosts has purposed, and who will annul it?
His hand is stretched out, and who will turn it back?***

***Isaiah 14:27***

Many of us spend a great deal of time talking about what the devil has stolen from us. We sometimes get caught up in what we used to have, and forget the One who is directing our lives today. I've come today to say that it's a set-up.

Many of us live in the past. We remember when we had money to pay our bills, before the kids. We remember when we started college and didn't finish. We remember when we had good jobs, and quit because we thought that the grass was greener on the other side. Know that if the devil has stolen something from you, then God opened the window for him. He opened the window because He knew that He could give you more through the door.

You see when we think about our lives, before the children, we fail to see the blessings that our children truly bring. Remember that if you are a parent, then you are blessed because there are many who are unable to conceive. There are many who would gladly pay the child support just to look down into the face of someone who looks just like them. There are many who pay thousands of dollars to try to conceive children, yet they can't. So look at the financial stress as a blessing. God is giving you a testimony. He has set you up for one of the most beautiful miracles that life offers and that is a child. Know that your set-up is a blessing from God.

It is never too late to go back to school. No one is too old to learn. It might be that you weren't meant to finish the first time. It might be that God knew you would not appreciate it in your youth. It might be that there is someone in a particular class that you are supposed to meet that is going to redirect your future. So stop blaming the devil and praise God. Know that nothing in life happens by chance. If the devil did it, then God allowed it. And if God allowed it, know that His Word says, "*no weapon formed against you shall prosper.*" You've been set-up by God to be blessed.

As Christians, we sometimes get confused about our jobs and their true intent. We think that our jobs are about us, when in actuality you are there to bring someone back to Christ. You are there to let your light shine. The world should be able to see you and know that a change in their life is necessary. It's not that you have to tell them to change, it's that you set an example so that they know they must change. If God has sent you to a certain place of employment, then hang in there until God releases you. Sometimes we leave prematurely and find that the grass is truly not greener on the other side. We find that what we left is actually better than where we went. Why? Because God's grace still covered your old job. So, move when He says move and stay when He says stay. Remember, you've been set-up by God to be blessed.

So today, as you spend time thinking about your life, remember to laugh at the devil because what he meant for evil, God is going to use for His good. Those turning points in life were really U-turns that God created to get you back on the right path. So stay focused on God and know that all windows that He allows to be closed are always covered by His grace on the doors that He will open. Stay strong and know that those things that appear to be set-backs are truly set-ups by God for you to be blessed.

## GOING BEYOND THE VEIL

***...but whenever Moses went in before the LORD to speak with him, he took the veil off, until he came out; and when he came out, and told the people of Israel what he was commanded***

***Exodus 34:34***

Do you ever go beyond the veil? I'm not talking about sitting and talking to God in your everyday prayer life. I'm talking about taking off your veil and entering His presence. Entering His presence with the understanding that when you exit He will send you forth with a mission.

As you go beyond the veil in life, know that it is through the presence of the anointing that makes it possible. Know that God has called you to do something great for Him in His Kingdom. Don't get confused and think that God can't use little old you. He used little old David. He used little old Daniel. He used little old Peter. He used little old Paul. He took little people and used them in a might way when they entered presence, to go beyond the veil.

As you go beyond the veil to seek God know that you must come out of all titles. You must go into His presence in worship of Him. Do you realize that you were born to worship Him? Do you know that your title in life does not determine your fortitude in His kingdom? To go beyond the veil and come away with answers is to enter His presence with thanksgiving and expectancy. To go beyond the veil, you must always enter His presence in reverence of His omnipotence and His majesty and His power. Expect that going beyond the veil could catapult you into a destiny where your only focus in life will be Jesus and the mission you are called to do.

So today, get ready to go beyond the veil. Take off your veil and enter His presence to see what He has to say to you. Leave the routine prayer behind. Go see what God has commanded you to do. For everyone in life, know that God has a purpose, a plan, and a provision. So remember, that *whenever Moses went in before the LORD to speak with him, he took the veil off, until he came out; and when he came out, and told the people of Israel what he was commanded.*

## About Our Author: Sheila T. Flowers

I speak from the innermost treasures of my soul as I reflect upon God's goodness and grace in my life. My spiritual journey is the most important thing in my life. I relocated to Atlanta from my home of Gainesville, FL and attended college at Florida A& M University. It was in these places that I felt I wanted something more than the material trappings that we can so easily fall into. I didn't know what that would be and I am still not sure that I have found the whole answer as of yet, but still I press on.

I pray that these inspirational thoughts have caused you to want to seek God in a more intimate way. I also pray that they have caused you to stop and give thought to whose you are in the Kingdom of God as well as made you want to search for God's intended purpose for your life. Remember you can do all things through Christ who strengthens you!

If you have been blessed by reading these thoughts I would love to hear from you. Please e-mail me at sflowers@aheartofflowers.com or write to me at P.O. Box 670 Austell, GA 30168.

And as always visit my website
http://www.aheartofflowers.com